"Now Show Them What Rhode Island Can Do!"

An Annotated Bibliography of Rhode Island Civil War Sources

Robert Grandchamp

HERITAGE BOOKS
2018

HERITAGE BOOKS
AN IMPRINT OF HERITAGE BOOKS, INC.

Books, CDs, and more—Worldwide

For our listing of thousands of titles see our website at
www.HeritageBooks.com

Published 2018 by
HERITAGE BOOKS, INC.
Publishing Division
5810 Ruatan Street
Berwyn Heights, Md. 20740

Copyright © 2018 Robert Grandchamp

Heritage Books by the author:

From Providence to Fort Hell: Letters from Company K, Seventh Rhode Island Volunteers
"Now Show Them What Rhode Island Can Do!": An Annotated Bibliography of Rhode Island Civil War Sources
"We Lost Many Brave Men": A Statistical History of the Seventh Rhode Island Volunteers
"With their usual ardor": Scituate, Rhode Island and the American Revolution

All rights reserved. No part of this book may be reproduced or transmitted in any form or by any means, electronic or mechanical, including photocopying, recording or by any information storage and retrieval system without written permission from the author, except for the inclusion of brief quotations in a review.

International Standard Book Number
Paperbound: 978-0-7884-5829-3

"Now Show Them What Rhode Island Can Do!:"

An Annotated Bibliography of

Rhode Island Civil War Sources

By:

Robert Grandchamp

"Now Show Them What Rhode Island Can Do!"

-Colonel John Stanton Slocum

Second Rhode Island Volunteers

July 21, 1861

For Elizabeth

CONTENTS

Introduction	1
Chapter One: General Sources	13
Chapter Two: Biographical Sources	27
Chapter Three: Rhode Island Militia Sources	41
Chapter Four: Infantry Sources	47
Chapter Five: Light Artillery Sources	77
Chapter Six: Heavy Artillery Sources	91
Chapter Seven: Cavalry Sources	101
Chapter Eight: Naval Sources	113
Chapter Nine: Veteran Sources	117
Chapter Ten: Town Histories	121
Chapter Eleven: Monuments and Cemeteries	131
Chapter Twelve: Conclusions	135
Acknowledgements	139
About the Author	141

Introduction

With the firing on Fort Sumter on April 12, 1861 Rhode Islanders eagerly answered the call to arms. From Westerly to Woonsocket, Wallum Lake to Little Compton, the men from Rhode Island went to war. When it was over the smallest state in the Union mustered eight regiments of infantry, three heavy artillery regiments, three regiments and a squadron of cavalry, ten batteries of light artillery, as well as hundreds of men who served in the United States Navy, Army, and Marine Corps. Rhode Islanders served in nearly every major battle of the war, firing the first infantry shots at Bull Run, and some of the last by the cavalry at Appomattox. Over 23,000 Rhode Islanders enlisted in the Civil War, over 2,000 gave the ultimate sacrifice.[1]

From 1862 until the second decade of the twentieth century, the soldiers and sailors of Rhode Island also left an indelible mark on the pages of history by writing and publishing many histories of their participation in the Civil War. Indeed, with the exception of Batteries C and G, First Rhode Island Light Artillery and the Second and Third Rhode Island Cavalry Regiments, every unit sent from Rhode Island published a history written by men who served in the organization. Over the last century these veteran published sources were added to by scores of other books and articles by scholars, buffs, and those interested in Rhode Island's role in the Civil War. Indeed, Rhode Island has perhaps the greatest written record of any northern state in the Civil War era.

In 1862, Augustus Woodbury published *A Narrative of the Campaign of the First Rhode Island Regiment in the Spring and Summer of 1861*. This book was the very first published regimental history written by a participant in the Civil War. Woodbury, who served in the First Rhode Island Detached Militia

---

[1] For a good overview of the Rhode Island Civil War experience, refer to Robert Grandchamp, *Rhode Island and the Civil War: Voices from the Ocean State.* (Charleston: History Press, 2012)

as the regimental chaplain set the gold standard by which all future regimental histories were and are written. He placed the role of the First Rhode Island within the context of the Bull Run Campaign and focused heavily on the participation of the regiment in the engagement. Woodbury included a complete roster of the First Rhode Island and included short biographies of the officers and men who perished in the service. As the war was still being fought, Woodbury also listed men from the regiment who had reenlisted in other units Woodbury's style of writing a regimental history would be repeated by nearly every other author in the decades ahead.[2]

In 1864, Edwin W. Stone, who served in Battery C, First Rhode Island Light Artillery, published *Rhode Island in the Rebellion*. During the war, Stone served as a correspondent to the *Providence Journal,* writing detailed letters about his experiences in the Army of the Potomac. The book was published in early 1864, and only contains Stone's letters written through Gettysburg. Despite this, *Rhode Island in the Rebellion* is a valuable resource. Nearly a third of book is an appendix in which are brief histories of each Rhode Island regiment and battery. Stone did not write these histories himself, rather a member of each unit wrote the history for inclusion in the book. These histories present a remarkable view of the war, as it was going on by the participants. In addition, Stone also included brief biographies of several Rhode Island soldiers who died in the war. *Rhode Island in the Rebellion* was reissued in 1865 with the inclusion of a chapter on the events of 1864 and additional biographical material for officers who died in the 1864 campaigns. Often overlooked today, *Rhode Island in the Rebellion* remains a valuable resource.[3]

Chaplain Woodbury returned to publishing in 1875 by writing the official regimental history of the Second Rhode Island Volunteers. For his work, Woodbury spoke with fellow veterans of the regiment, and was freely given access to both private and

---

[2] *Newport Mercury,* June 21, 1862.
[3] Edwin M. Stone, *Rhode Island in the Rebellion*. (Providence: George H. Whitney, 1864 and 1865)

personal papers of the soldiers of the Second. The *Providence Journal* recorded, "The historian understood that nothing but the truth and impartiality was sought, and from such a man nothing else could have been obtained, even desired. The narrative is sprightly and told in Mr. Woodbury's happiest style." Chaplain Frederic Denison who served in both the First Rhode Island Cavalry and the Third Rhode Island Heavy Artillery published *Sabres and Spurs* and *Shot and Shell* in 1876 and 1879 respectively. Denison, a Brown University educated Baptist minister of the "church militant" was also a historian who wrote two excellent histories which are widely considered to still be two of the best sources on the cavalry in the Army of the Potomac, and service in South Carolina. A poet as well, Denison published his poetry in these volumes.[4]

One of the most important sources published by Rhode Islanders was the one hundred papers published in the ten volumes of the *Personal Narratives of Events in the War of the Rebellion: Being papers read before the Rhode Island Soldiers and Sailors Historical Society*. Formed in Providence in 1874, the Soldiers and Sailors Historical Society was composed of veterans who met each month where one of the members would present a historical paper on their military service. One hundred of these papers were issued in paperback form from 1878 until 1915, shortly after which the society disbanded. The *New England Historical and Genealogical Register* recorded, "The society deserves much credit for its labors in preserving the record of events in so important a portion of our national history."

The papers were collected and published in hardcover in volumes of ten papers, comprising ten full volumes. Publishing the single volumes received praise. "They contain much interesting matter concerning events in the late war for the preservation of the union, which but for this mode of publication would have been

---

[4] *Providence Journal*, March 17, 1875. Frederic Denison, *Sabres and Spurs: The First Regiment Rhode Island Cavalry in the Civil War, 1861-1865. Its Origins, Marches, Scouts, Skirmishes, Raid, Battles, Sufferings, Victories, and Appropriate Official Papers; with The Roll of Honor and Roll of the Regiment.* (Central Falls: E.L. Freeman, 1876)

lost." It is important to note that not all papers read before the Society were published as many still exist in manuscript form at the Rhode Island Historical Society and Providence Public Library, while others were independently published elsewhere by their authors.

The full set of ten volumes was republished in the 1990s by Broadfoot Publishing as part of their series of war papers from the Military Order of the Loyal Legion of the United States (MOLLUS). Despite this, these papers were not published originally by MOLLUS and Rhode Island never had a MOLLUS Commandery. In addition to this, not all of the papers were written by men who served in Rhode Island units. Because these papers were initially issued individually, they will be listed under the regiments in which their author served.[5]

Prior to 1892, Rhode Islanders had sporadically published sources about their participation in the war. The histories published before were published by and paid for entirely by the veterans or the regimental association. Often published in limited numbers, these books were found in the many mill village libraries throughout the state. In 1890, the veterans of the Fifth Rhode Island Heavy Artillery sent a resolution to the Rhode Island General Assembly asking for a sum of money to help in writing and publishing a regimental history. Beginning in 1892, the Rhode Island General Assembly offered each Rhode Island regimental veteran association six hundred dollars to publish a regimental history of their unit. The state would purchase two hundred copies of the history "for the use of the state," often sending them to libraries both in Rhode Island and elsewhere, as well as to veteran's homes and Grand Army of the Republic Posts around the country. In addition, members of the General Assembly and judges of the Rhode Island court system were also given copies to give to their constituents. The generous gift of the Rhode Island

---

[5] Finding Aid, Rhode Island Soldiers and Sailors Historical Society Papers, MSS 723, Rhode Island Historical Society, Providence, RI. "Book Notices." *The New England Historical and Genealogical Register* Vol. 36 (1882), 100-101. "Book Notices." *The New England Historical and Genealogical* Register Vol. 35 (1881), 406.

General Assembly was the catalyst for the remaining Rhode Island veteran associations to publish regimental histories.[6]

Typical of these histories is the massive 1903 regimental history of the Seventh Rhode Island Volunteers. Raised in 1862, the Seventh saw hard service in both the Army of the Potomac and in Mississippi during the Vicksburg Campaign. The soldiers of the Seventh formed a veteran association in 1873, but did not begin to seriously consider writing a regimental history until 1889 when a committee of twenty-five veterans gathered to write the history. "A committee of so many members was found to be unwieldy and inefficient and accomplished little of importance," wrote one member of the regiment. By 1893, the twenty-five-member committee had accomplished little work in writing the history. Instead, Seventh Rhode Island Veteran Association president, Nathan B. Lewis who had served in the regiment as a corporal and was now a prominent lawyer and judge in Washington County appointed another committee of five members to gather funds to publish the history to supplement the money provided by the state. William P. Hopkins, a former drummer in the regiment was appointed to write the actual history.

Hopkins, now living in Lawrence, Massachusetts was "indefatigable in collecting material for such a work." He wrote thousands of letters to fellow veterans, including Confederates that the Seventh fought against, gathered letters and diaries of fellow veterans from the Seventh, collected hundreds of photographs of regimental comrades, and wrote biographical sketches of most of the soldiers in the regiment. Furthermore, Hopkins traveled throughout the South, revisiting the battlefields the Seventh had fought and camped on in Maryland, Virginia, and Mississippi. By the time he was done his research, which took up most of the

---

[6] John K. Burlingame, *History of the Fifth Regiment of Rhode Island Heavy Artillery During Three Years and a Half of Service in North Carolina. January 1862-June 1865.* (Providence: Snow & Farnum, 1892), v-viii. *Acts and Resolves Passed by the General Assembly of the State of Rhode Island and Providence Plantations at the January Session, 1899.* (Providence: E.L. Freeman, 1899), 221-222.

1890s, Hopkins "had sufficient material to make a credible history of the regiment."

Hopkins wrote his history of the Seventh Rhode Island and had it edited by Dr. George B. Peck of Providence, himself a veteran of the Second Rhode Island and author of several accounts of his own service. Hopkins wrote, "The result sought in the publication of this volume is to place on record an authentic account of the part performed by the Seventh Rhode Island Regiment in the suppression of the Rebellion and to perpetuate the memory of the heroic men who gave up their lives in the service of their country." When it was published in 1903, *The Seventh Regiment Rhode Island Volunteers in the Civil War, 1862-1865* was widely hailed, and still is, as one of the finest regimental histories published in the post-war period. Filled with hundreds of photographs, biographical sketches, and a main text that reads like a diary from a front-line participant, it is one of the greatest books ever published on Rhode Island in the Civil War era.[7]

The First Rhode Island Light Artillery regiment was unique in its service. Recruited at the Benefit Street Arsenal in Providence, the eight batteries of the regiment were mustered in one battery at a time and never served together as a full regiment. One veteran jokingly referred to the First Rhode Island Light Artillery as a "geography class" because of its varied service. In July 1863, Batteries A, B, C, E, and G were serving in the Army of the Potomac at Gettysburg. Battery D was stationed in Kentucky with the Ninth Corps, while Battery F was detailed to New Bern, North Carolina, and Battery H served in the defenses of Washington, D.C. Because of the wide and varied service of these batteries, each unit was authorized to publish a history; all did with the exception of Battery C and Battery G.[8]

---

[7] Seventh Rhode Island Volunteers, Regimental Association Minute Books, 1885-1903, Robert Grandchamp Collection. William P. Hopkins, *The Seventh Regiment Rhode Island Volunteers in the Civil War, 1862-1865*. (Providence: Snow & Farnum, 1903), i-xvi.

[8] George B. Peck, *Historical Address Delivered at the Dedication of the Memorial Tablet on the Arsenal Benefit Street, Corner of Meeting Providence, R.I. Thursday July 19, 1917*. (Providence: Rhode Island Print Co., 1917), 5-15.

Taken together, these regimental histories form one of the most important resources to study Rhode Island in the Civil War period. Written by the men who participated in the unit, they present a detailed, first-hand account of their service. Furthermore, many of the volumes contain engravings or photographs of the officers and men who served in the unit. Of particular importance are biographical sketches and accounts of the actions in which they participated. Sometimes though, it must be remembered that these sources were written after the Civil War, in the Gilded Age, and often do not discuss desertions, the high bounties that some men enlisted for, and drunk or incompetent officers. While some of these regimental histories do have their shortcomings in not discussing the dark side of the war, for the most part they provide an honest, day to day view of Rhode Island's Civil War units. The books were widely distributed and varied in cost upon publication, the history of Battery B sold for three dollars, while the history of the Seventh Rhode Island Volunteers originally sold for five dollars. The men who wrote these books often spent more on their publication than what they made in sales. It was a labor of love that led them to recall their unit's part in the Civil War.[9]

After 1917, with the disbandment of the Rhode Island Soldiers and Sailors Historical Society and the passing of many of the state's Civil War veterans, the steady stream of publications about Rhode Island and the Civil War began to decline. In 1964, Brigadier General Harold R. Barker, a veteran of both World Wars whose grandfather had served in the First Rhode Island Detached Militia wrote, *History of Rhode Island Combat Units in the Civil War* which served as the official state history to commemorate the Centennial of the Civil War. General Barker's book is a compression of the regimental histories published by the veterans after the war. He performed no original research, rather publishing excerpts from the histories to detail the role of a Rhode Island unit in a particular battle. The book is heavily illustrated and also includes details such as Medal of Honor recipients, and the battle honors earned by each regiment. Widely distributed by the state,

---

[9] Advertisement for Battery B, First Rhode Island Light Artillery Regimental History, Gettysburg National Military Park, Gettysburg, PA. *Publisher's Weekly,* April 4, 1903. *Providence Evening Press,* July 21, 1871.

General Barker's book is still frequently read and is often the first book many read on Rhode Island and the Civil War.[10]

It was not until the 1980s that another round of books on Rhode Island and the Civil War were published. In 1985, Robert Hunt Rhodes, the great-grandson of Colonel Elisha Hunt Rhodes of the Second Rhode Island Volunteers published his ancestor's diary through Mowbray Publishing in Woonsocket as *All For the Union*. This book is a publication of the fair copy of Rhodes' diary which he recopied after the war, and differs in some places from his field journal kept during the war, especially in his opinions of the Union high command. The book was not widely known until Rhodes' neighbor in New Hampshire, Ken Burns bought a copy. Burns used Elisha Hunt Rhodes as the archetypical Union soldier in his 1990 series *The Civil War*. *All For the Union* was republished in paperback by Random House, selling tens of thousands of copies, and becoming the most widely read book about Rhode Island and the Civil War.

In the early 1990s, Kris VanDenBossche, an antiques dealer from Hopkinton formed the Rhode Island Historical Document Transcription Project. He traveled the state seeking out documents and photographs for inclusion in a project sponsored by the Rhode Island Council of the Humanities. VanDenBossche gathered hundreds of letters and transcribed them for publication. His book, *Pleas Excuse All Bad Writing* was distributed to every library in Rhode Island and not made available for sale to the general public. A companion volume, *Write Soon and Give Me All The News* is found at the Rhode Island Historical Society. These books are two of the best and most available sources of letters written by Rhode Island soldiers.[11]

In 1996 Butternut & Blue, a Maryland based publisher of Civil War books reissued the histories of the First Rhode Island

---

[10] Harold R. Barker, *History of the Rhode Island Combat Units in the Civil War (1861-1865)*. Providence: NP, 1964. Harold R. Barker Papers, Rhode Island Historical Society and Benefit Street Arsenal, Providence, RI.
[11] *Standard Times,* April 8, 1992. *Westerly Sun,* May 23, 1993. *Westerly Sun,* August 2, 1992.

Cavalry and Battery B, First Rhode Island Light Artillery as part of their Army of the Potomac Series. These two republications featured an extensive introduction about both units written by Robert Durwood Madison, a native Rhode Islander and then professor of history at the United States Naval Academy. With the advent of newer, cheaper, publishing technologies, companies such as Higginson Books in Salem, Massachusetts began to reissue reprints of regimental histories. Previously only available at libraries or for hefty sums from rare book dealers, these reprints made the regimental histories available to the public again. With the emergence of a renewed interest in the Civil War beginning in the late 1980s and the founding of the Rhode Island Civil War Round Table, reenacting groups such as Battery B and the Second Rhode Island, as well as a surge of membership in the Rhode Island Sons of Union Veterans, there was a renewed interest in the history of Rhode Island and the Civil War era, which led to a spate of new publications.

Perhaps the greatest contribution to the historiography of Rhode Island and the Civil War era has been made by Robert Grandchamp. A twelfth generation Rhode Islander, Grandchamp, at an early age discovered that his third great uncle, Alfred Sheldon Knight had served and died in the service as a member of Company C, Seventh Rhode Island Volunteers. Inspired by his ancestor's service, he took an active interest in the overall history of Rhode Island and the Civil War in high school that eventually took him to Rhode Island College where he earned an M.A. in American history. Grandchamp believed firmly in conducting in-depth, primary research on the Civil War by visiting every historical society, archive, and library in the state, as well as visiting nearly every Civil War era graveyard in Rhode Island. Furthermore, he has traveled the country, visiting museums, libraries, and battlefields gathering material from out of state sources on Rhode Island participation. In addition, he actively collected and continues to collect books, artifacts, and manuscript material on Rhode Island military history.

In his twenty years of research, Grandchamp has come to be widely considered as the nation's foremost authority on Rhode

Island military history. He is often consulted by the Rhode Island National Guard, the Varnum Continentals, Kentish Guards, and other organizations for his expertise in military history. During his college years, from 2008-2011 he was the lead researcher and writer on a history of the Providence Marine Corps of Artillery and the 103rd Field Artillery of the Rhode Island National Guard. Grandchamp served as a National Park Ranger at Harpers Ferry and Shenandoah. This experience led to many contacts in the historical community that can be tapped as needed. In 2012, Robert researched and led a program as part of Rhode Island Day at Antietam National Battlefield.

Robert's work has been published in a wide variety of national and local magazines and journals. He is a frequent contributor to *Rhode Island Roots,* published by the Rhode Island Genealogical Society. Furthermore, in 2017 he published a controversial article in *America's Civil War* magazine that established that Sullivan Ballou did not write the famous last letter made famous in Ken Burns' *Civil War* series. In addition, he has authored a dozen books for which he received letters of commendation from Governor Lincoln Chaffee and Mayor Angel Tavares of Providence. Furthermore, he became the first civilian recipient of the Order of St. Barbara from the Rhode Island National Guard for his contributions to the history of the Rhode Island artillery community. Among Grandchamp's writings are regimental histories of the Seventh Rhode Island Volunteers and Battery G, First Rhode Island Light Artillery. He has edited the correspondence of several Rhode Island soldiers, co-authored a bi-centennial history of the Providence Marine Corps of Artillery, and wrote the popular book, *Rhode Island and the Civil War: Voices from the Ocean State.*

In addition to Robert Grandchamp's work, the Sesquicentennial of the Civil War, commemorated from 2011-2015, also saw several other publications. Although widely known as a Lincoln scholar, Judge Frank Williams, the chair of the state committee for the Sesquicentennial edited a book about the contributions of those Rhode Islanders who remained at home during the war. Frank Grzyb, a Vietnam veteran and retired government employee wrote *Hidden History of Rhode Island and the Civil War* and *Rhode Island's Civil War Hospital: Life and Death at Portsmouth Grove*. Most recently the East Providence Historical Society released *All Quiet on the Rappahannock Tonight,* which is a compilation of the letters of Lieutenant Peter Hunt of Battery A who was mortally wounded at Cold Harbor. The conclusion of this book will discuss the future of publications about Rhode Island and the Civil War.

In the pages that follow, this editor has endeavored to gather and read *every* known *published* source pertaining to Rhode Island and the Civil War era. Each source has been cited using Turabian Style, which is the standard used by American historians. For obvious reasons, manuscript material has been excepted from this publication. Thousands of letters written by Rhode Island soldiers and sailors rest in repositories around the state, such as at the Rhode Island Historical Society, John Hay Library at Brown University, the Newport Historical Society, and the Varnum Museum in East Greenwich. The Rhode Island State Archives in Providence is the official repository for the government records of Rhode Island, while the Westerly Public Library maintains a remarkable Grand Army of the Republic and Civil War collection in their special collections.

Also excepted from listing are the various pieces of ephemera produced for regimental reunions, monument dedications, and other special events. The books, pamphlets, thesis, and monographs contained within this book were published and directly relate to the experience of Rhode Island and the Civil War era. These volumes are available to the public at many of the larger libraries in Rhode Island, the Providence Public Library, John Hay Library, or the Rhode Island Historical Society. In addition, many can now be found online in digital form on Google Books.

The tomes below are organized by general works, regimental type, and town histories. Each book or other publication has been carefully reviewed by this editor and its historical value has been annotated for each entry. Taken as a whole, this volume represents *every known* published volume relating to Rhode Island and the Civil War published between 1862 and 2018.

Chapter One:

General Sources

Achtermier, William O. *Rhode Island Arms Makers & Gunsmiths: 1643-1883*. Providence: Man at Arms, 1980.

During the Civil War, Rhode Island's textile based economy rapidly expanded to produce arms for the Union cause. The Mansfield & Lamb scythe works in Smithfield began producing cavalry sabers, while the Providence Tool Company and Burnside Rifle Company made firearms. This book details the history of firearms manufacturing in Rhode Island, with a focus on the Providence Tool Company.

Barker, Harold R. *History of the Rhode Island Combat Units in the Civil War (1861-1865)*. Providence: NP, 1964.

As stated in the introduction, this book was written by General Barker in the early 1960s for the Centennial celebration of the Civil War. It provides a good overview of the role of Rhode Island units in the different battles of the war, as well as illustrations of the different commanders of these units. This highly readable book places each Rhode Island unit within the context of the battle it was engaged in. A very good introductory study.

Bartlett, John Russell. *Memoirs of Rhode Island Officers, Who Were Engaged in the Service of Their Country During the Great Rebellion of the South: Illustrated with Thirty-Four Portraits*. Providence: Sidney S. Rider, 1867.

One of the best and most important books ever written about Rhode Island and the Civil War. Begun by Secretary of State John Russell Bartlett, a noted bibliophile who began collecting books on the Civil War immediately after the conflict started, this volume contains biographies of every Rhode Island officer who commanded a regiment or battery during the Civil War. Even more important are the biographies of those officers who died in the conflict; these sketches were written by family members and include many fine quotations from their private letters. The book is also enhanced by thirty-four engravings of the officers.

Belanger, Claude and Damien Belanger. "Franco-Americans in the Civil War Era." *Je Me Souviens* Vol. 26, No. 2 (Autumn 2003), 19-49.

A very detailed article regarding the history of Quebecois soldiers joining the Union forces during the Civil War, focusing on their motivations for joining. The authors focus on Rhode Island and the other New England states. Between 20,000 and 40,000 Quebecois served in the United States forces during the Civil War.

Branigan, George. "Letters to the Providence Reform School." *Rhode Island Roots* Vol. 34, No. 3 (September 2008), 142-156.

An interesting article about the Providence Reform School. Many of the teenage inmates sent there during the Civil War were given the choice of remaining incarcerated or joining the service; many of them did. Branigan traces the history of the school and includes several transcriptions of students who served in the Union army.

Burrage, Henry S. *Brown University in the Civil War: A Memorial.* Providence: Providence Press Co., 1868.

This book is a memorial volume to honor the alumni of Brown University who died in the Civil War. Each soldier is commemorated by a biographical sketch written by someone who knew the soldier. Contains a wealth of information on men who served in Rhode Island units, as it frequently includes quotes from their private letters. In addition, an appendix includes a list of all Brown University alumni who served in the Union forces.

Cady, John Hutchins. *Rhode Island Boundaries: 1636-1936.* Providence: Rhode Island Tercentenary Commission, 1936.

A must-read book to understand the physical boundaries during the Civil War era. The town boundaries of the state have changed dramatically since the Civil War; as such this book provides important information regarding the geography of Rhode Island during the Civil War era.

Chapin, Howard M. *Illustrations of the Seals, Arms, and Flags of Rhode Island.* Providence: Rhode Island Historical Society, 1930.

An interesting book about the development of the Rhode Island flag. This book provides rare illustrations of Rhode Island battle flags and town emblems.

Coleman, Peter. *The Transformation of Rhode Island, 1790-1860.* Westport: Greenwood Press, 1985.

In the period between the American Revolution to the Civil War, Rhode Island transformed from an economy based largely on trade with the sea to becoming one of the most developed, urbanized, and economically important states in the North. Coleman's book traces this development and provides an important view into Antebellum Rhode Island.

Clark-Pujara, Christy. "The Business of Slavery and Antislavery Sentiment: The Case of Rowland Gibson Hazard- An Antislavery 'Negro Cloth' Dealer." *Rhode Island History* Vol. 71 No. 2 (Summer/Fall 2013), 35-56.

Prior to the Civil War the economy of Rhode Island was directly linked to the South, with many Rhode Island mills using southern cotton to create fabric, or in the case of Hazard's South Kingstown mills, cloth for slave owners to cloth their slaves in. Although he was against the slave trade, and an abolitionist, Hazard's mills produced much of the cloth used in the South. An interesting article about how Rhode Island's economy was linked to the South.

Conley, Patrick T. *Democracy in Decline: Rhode Island's Constitutional Development, 1776-1841.* Providence: Rhode Island Historical Society, 1988.

The best political history written about Rhode Island, Conley, a long-time history professor at Providence College traces the origins of the Dorr Rebellion and the development of politics in Rhode Island. Very useful for understanding the politics of Rhode Island in the years leading up to the Civil War.

Dailey, Charlotte F. *Report Upon the Disabled Rhode Island Soldiers: Their Names, Condition, and in What Hospital They Are. Made to His Excellency Gov. Sprague, and Presented to the General Assembly of Rhode Island, January Session, 1863.* Providence: A. Anthony, 1863.

Following the Battle of Fredericksburg in January 1863, Governor Sprague sent Charlotte Dailey of Providence to Washington to visit each hospital to find and identify Rhode Island soldiers needing treatment. Dailey found nearly 500 Rhode Islanders suffering from wounds or illness requiring treatment; this is the report of her findings and provides a detailed view of the sufferings endured by Rhode Island's soldiers.

Delisle, Paul. "Rhode Island Franco-Canadians in the Civil War." *Je Me Souviens* Vol. 15, No. 1 (Spring 1992), 6-42.

Although the vast majority of Quebecois (French-Canadian) immigration did not arrive in Rhode Island until after the Civil War, a good number of them did serve in Rhode Island units. Delisle's article, published in the journal of the Woonsocket based American-French Genealogical Society provides a list of men in Rhode Island units documented as having Quebecois ancestry.

Duchesneau, John T. and Kathleen Troost-Cramer. *Fort Adams: A History.* Charleston: History Press, 2014.

Duchesneau, John T. and Kathleen Troost-Cramer. *True Tales of Life & Death at Fort Adams*. Charleston, SC: The History Press, 2013

Built to guard the entrance to Narragansett Bay and Newport harbor, Fort Adams is one of the largest masonry forts in the United States. During the Civil War it served as a training and recruiting ground for the United States Army. In these two books, the authors chronicle the history of Fort Adams from the War of 1812 through the modern period, as well as providing a harrowing narrative of men who died while on service at Fort Adams. Duchesneau is a veteran of the Rhode Island National Guard with multiple deployments to Iraq. Two excellent volumes.

Dyer, Elisha. *Annual Report of the Adjutant General of the State of Rhode Island and Providence Plantations, for the Year 1865*. Two Volumes. Providence: E.L. Freeman & Sons, 1893.

More commonly referred to as the *Revised Register of Rhode Island Volunteer,* this massive two volume set is the single most important book ever published about Rhode Island and the Civil War. Beginning in the 1880s, Adjutant General Elisha Dyer, himself a Civil War veteran and Rhode Island's first Civil War casualty began the massive project "to perfect, restore, copy, and preserve the military records of the State." Combing through thousands of muster rolls and corresponding with veterans, Dyer and his small team produced a massive two volume set listing every soldier, sailor, and Marine who served from Rhode Island. Volume One contains men who served in the infantry, while Volume Two is a listing of men in the cavalry, artillery, and the Regulars, as well as the U.S. Navy and Marine Corps. Each man's enlistment record is listed, as is any pertinent casualty information. The book also contains brief histories of each Rhode Island unit, as well as documents from the Rhode Island Adjutant General's office. Although the work is far from complete, as Dyer often did not list men who came home and died as a direct result of their Civil War service after being mustered out, this book is a comprehensive list of the service and sacrifice of Rhode Island's veterans.

Gavitt, Edward G. *Rhode Island in the Civil War: Through the real life experiences of the men who fought it.* Bristol, CT: The Author, 1997.

An interesting self-published book. This volume came out in the late 1990s and is a history of the Gavitt family during the Civil War. The author does a good job of providing a general overview of the Rhode Island Civil War experience throughout the text. Of importance, however is the inclusion of several letters written by Gavitt family members during the Civil War from those who served in the Seventh and Twelfth Rhode Island Volunteers, as well as Battery F. The Gavitt family hailed largely from the Westerly area, with another branch in Coventry. The book was never sold or marketed and is available at some of the larger libraries in Rhode Island.

George, Robert H. "Brown University on the Eve of the Civil War." *Books at Brown* Vol. XX (1965), 1-18.

George, Robert H. "Brunonians in Confederate Ranks, 1861-1865." *Books at Brown* Vol. XX (1965), 19-34.

History professor Robert H. George of Brown University spent much of the early 1960s collecting materials for a planned book on Rhode Island and the Civil War. The book was never published, but his research notes are today housed at the Brown University Archives at the John Hay Library in Providence. These two articles are based on George's research. He chronicles the social conditions at the University in 1860-1861 through the letters of men who later went to war. In addition, he compiled a list of the Brown alumni who served in the Confederate forces.

Grandchamp, Robert. *Rhode Island and the Civil War: Voices from the Ocean State.* Charleston: History Press, 2012.

Published as a companion piece for the Civil War Sesquicentennial, Grandchamp's book is a readable, highly illustrated, and detailed account of each Rhode Island regiment and battery sent to the front. Appendices include a list of Medal of Honor recipients from Rhode Island, as well as the letters of several soldiers. This book is highly recommended for all ages, as well as those just beginning their research into Rhode Island and the Civil War.

Grandchamp, Robert. "Rhode Island Uniforms in the Civil War." *Military Images* Vol. 28, No. 5(May/June 2007), 28-32.

A detailed analysis of the many different styles of uniforms worn by different Rhode Island regiments during the Civil War. Includes images of men from different Rhode Island units.

Grzyb, Frank L. *Hidden History of Rhode Island and the Civil War*. Charleston: History Press, 2013.

A colorful potpourri of Rhode Island Civil War stories and anecdotes. This book is both entertaining and enlightening and is highly readable.

Grzyb, Frank L. *Rhode Island's Civil War Hospital: Life and Death at Portsmouth Grove, 1862-1865*. Jefferson, N.C.: McFarland, 2012.

Founded in 1862, the Civil War hospital at Portsmouth Grove, located north of Newport became one of the largest treatment centers in the North for recovering Union soldiers. In this original work, Grzyb conducted in-depth research to tell the full story of the hospital. He focuses on the medical staff, the guards, as well as the patients treated there. A detailed work that is the best study for this important part of Civil War history.

Harrington, Peter S. "Anne S.K. Brown." *Books at Brown* Vol. XL (1998), 1-13.

The Anne S.K. Brown military collection at the John Hay Library is a remarkable collection of militaria from around the world. Among the many items in the collection is a large grouping of letters and artifacts from Rhode Island Civil War soldiers. This article chronicles the development of the collection.

Hayman, Robert W. "The Rhode Island Irish and the Civil War." *Rhode Island History* Vol. 73, No. 2 (Summer/Fall, 2015), 46-67.

A detailed article by a professor at Providence College. Hayman analyzes the Irish experience in Rhode Island during the Civil War such as recruiting and soldier relief work. He focuses on the attempts to raise an all Irish regiment that ultimately failed; the Third Rhode Island Heavy Artillery contained the most Irish of any unit. In addition to this, Hayman researches how Irish veterans attempted to use their service to gain suffrage after the war.

Hoar, Jay S. *New England's Last Civil War Veterans*. Arlington, TX: Seacliff Press, 1976.

A professor from Maine, Hoar spent much of his life chronicling the last surviving Civil War veterans in the 1930s-1950s, some of whom he met as a teenager. This book includes a roster and biographies of the last men to have worn the Union blue from Rhode Island.

Hoffman, Charles and Tess Hoffman. *North By South: The Two Lives of Richard James Arnold*. Athens: University of Georgia Press, 1988.

A member of the Providence elite, Richard Arnold lived a double life. He owned a large plantation in Georgia where he spent his winters, while summering in Newport. Arnold married into a slave holding family and became a slave holder and plantation owner. This book chronicles Arnold's life in Rhode Island and in Georgia as a rice and cotton planter. During the Civil War, Arnold remained in Rhode Island, while his two sons fought in a Georgia regiment. His plantation was not burned during Sherman's March to the Sea, and Arnold returned there after the war. A highly researched and detailed narrative, this book reveals the deep ties Rhode Island had with the South before the Civil War.

Hunt, Roger D. *Colonels in Blue: The New England States: Connecticut, Maine, Massachusetts, New Hampshire, Rhode Island, Vermont.* Atglen, PA: Schiffer Military History, 2001. Pp. 180-193.

This book is an important compilation of all the men who held the rank of colonel in each Rhode Island regiment during the Civil War. Hunt provides biographical sketches of each colonel, as well as at least one photograph of each man. An important desk reference book.

Miller, Richard F. *States at War: Volume I. A Reference Guide for Connecticut, Maine, Massachusetts, New Hampshire, Rhode Island, and Vermont in the Civil War.* Hanover: University Press of New England, 2013.

This interesting reference volume provides a detailed overview of political, military, and economic events in Rhode Island during the Civil War. Also included are abstract reports of the Rhode Island General Assembly, as well as state financial information. Miller also includes a timeline for key events that occurred in Rhode Island during the Civil War. Furthermore, he provides information regarding the Rhode Island Congressional delegation, as well as local politics in the state during the war. This thick reference volume provides details on the overall situation in Rhode Island. A very informative source.

Morton, Lloyd. *Report on the Physical Condition of the Rhode Island Regiments, Now in the Field, in Virginia and in the Vicinity of Washington, D.C. Also on the Condition of the Hospitals in and Around Washington.* Providence: A. Anthony, 1863.

Following the Battle of Fredericksburg, Governor Sprague sent Dr. Morton, a Providence physician to Virginia to inspect the condition of the Rhode Island units in the field. Morton visited each camp and wrote this important report. Many Union soldiers compared the winter of 1862-1863 as being similar to the Valley Forge winter during the American Revolution. This report reflects the terrible condition of the Rhode Island units following Fredericksburg where many struggled to survive a constant battle against disease and the elements.

Ray, John Michael. "Rhode Island Reactions to John Brown's Raid." *Rhode Island History* Vol. 20, No. 4 (October 1961), 97-108.

Although many causes led to the Civil War, after the abortive October 1859 raid at Harpers Ferry by the radical abolitionist John Brown there was no going back. In this detailed article, Ray details the reaction in Rhode Island to Brown's Raid. Unlike the rest of New England that was sympathetic to his cause, Ray details, through newspaper articles and letters that the majority of Rhode Islanders, with the exception of those living in the Woonsocket area condemned Brown's actions and did not participate in a nationwide ringing of bells when he was executed. A very interesting article.

Report of Finance Committee of the House of Representatives, on Bounty Frauds, &C.: Made at the January Session, 1865. Providence: H.H. Thomas & Co., 1865.

This important work chronicles the tremendous fraud involving bounties paid to Rhode Island soldiers late in the war. It includes the report of the committee, as well as the testimony of several Rhode Island soldiers who were cheated out of their bounties by recruiting officers, especially important is the testimony of several men from the Fourteenth Rhode Island. Despite the investigation, little was done to repay the bounties owed to the men of the Fourteenth which was swindled by several officers in the regiment.

Rhode Island Civil War Chronicles. No. 1 (December 1960).

Originally envisioned as a quarterly journal covering Rhode Island's participation in the Civil War Centennial 1961-1965, due to a lack of funding, only one volume of this interesting little journal was printed. This single volume provides some interesting details on various aspects of Rhode Island and the Civil War.

Rolston, Les. *Lost Soul: The Confederate Soldier in New England*. Orem, UT: Ancestry, 1999.

In the early 1990s, Rolston discovered a Confederate soldier, Samuel Postlethwaite of the 21st Mississippi buried in Coventry. This book is a biography of this soldier, as well as Rolston's efforts to mark his grave. Despite Rolston's claims, Postlethwaite is not the only Confederate veteran buried in Rhode Island.

Silber, Nina, and Mary Beth Sievens. *Yankee Correspondence: Civil War Letters between New England Soldiers and the Home Front*. Charlottesville: University Press of Virginia, 1996.

This interesting volume contains the correspondence of soldiers from all six New England states, as well as a detailed narrative regarding the wartime experience of New Englanders. Containing the letters of several Rhode Islanders, this book is a very informative source for regional information.

Smith, James Y. *Special Message of His Excellency James Y. Smith, Governor of Rhode Island, to the General Assembly, January, 1866*. Providence: Providence Press Co., 1866.

This interesting report, submitted to the Rhode Island General Assembly by Governor Smith is a chronological breakdown of all the expenses incurred by the State of Rhode Island during the Civil War in raising and equipping troops. A very detailed report to understanding how the Rhode Island government spent money during the Civil War.

Stone, Edwin W. *Rhode Island in the Rebellion.* Providence: G.H. Whitney, 1865.

Originally published in 1864, the 1865 reprint includes a major addendum. Stone served in Battery C and wrote frequent letters to the *Providence Journal* about his service. This book includes brief, but detailed histories of each Rhode Island unit, as well as biographies of some Rhode Islanders who died in the conflict. A very important source for information on Rhode Island in the Civil War.

Tremblay, Remi. *One Came Back: A Franco-American Civil War Novel.* Translated and Edited by Margaret S. Langford and Claire Quintal. Bennington, VT: Images from the Past, 2002.

Originally written in French and published in Quebec, this novel accurately recounts the Quebecois experience in the Civil War. A journalist, Tremblay enlisted in Rhode Island in the Fourteenth United States Infantry and served in the conflict. A remarkable story, based on his own wartime experiences, *One Came Back* follows two Quebecois soldiers through their Civil War experiences.

Van Broekhoven, Deborah Bingham. *The Devotion of These Women: Rhode Island in the Antislavery Network.* Amherst: University of Massachusetts Press, 2002.

In the years leading up to the Civil War, Rhode Island, especially the Blackstone Valley became a hotbed of abolitionism. In this study, retired professor Van Broekhoven details the role that Rhode Island women played in the struggle to free the slaves. She writes that after the anti-slavery movement all but collapsed after the Dorr Rebellion, a few devoted women kept the movement alive, corresponding with national leaders such as Garrison and Douglas. Their work ensured that Rhode Island continued hosting antislavery meeting and producing literature for the cause. An expertly researched monograph.

VanDenBossche, Kris. *"Pleas Excuse All Bad Writing:" A Documentary History of Rhode Island During the Civil War Era 1854-1865.* Peace Dale: Rhode Island Historical Document Transcription Project, 1993.

One of the finest books written about Rhode Island and the Civil War, VanDenBossche distributed copies of this book to every public library in Rhode Island as part of a grant from the Rhode Island Council for the Humanities. In this volume, he provides a compilation of letters written by Rhode Island soldiers from several different units and communities, as well as photographs. A critical resource to studying Rhode Island in the Civil War era.

VanDenBossche, Kris. *"Write Soon and Give Me All the News:" A Documentary History of Rhode Island During the Civil War Era.* Peace Dale: Rhode Island Historical Document Transcription Project, 1993.

In 1993, after VanDenBossche had distributed *Pleas Excuse All Bad Writing* to the libraries of Rhode Island, he compiled the remainder of his transcriptions into this volume. Much as the original volume, this contains the transcripts and notes regarding many of the soldiers who served in different Rhode Island regiments. A very important source of information. VanDenBossche distributed copies to the Rhode Island Historical Society.

Williams, Frank J. and Patrick T. Conley. *The Rhode Island Home Front in the Civil War Era.* Nashua: Taos Press, 2013.

The only published work of the Rhode Island Civil War Sesquicentennial Commission, this book provides a glimpse into how the Civil War directly affected those who remained behind in Rhode Island. The authors cover the economic impact on the state, as well as the social impact of the Irish-American response to the war.

Wilson, Joe Harvey. "Soldier Relief work in Rhode Island during the Civil War." M.A. Thesis, Brown University, 1931.

A relatively small master's thesis researched at Brown University in the 1930s. This work chronicles the roles of the Sanitary Commission, as well as the Christian Commission in Rhode Island during the war, with a focus on their work at Portsmouth Grove Hospital. A native of Texas, Harvey later obtained a doctorate in history and went on to become a college administrator in Texas.

Zambarano, Anthony L. "The Industrial Developments in Rhode Island During the Civil War Era." M.A. Thesis, University of Rhode Island, 1957.

A detailed M.A. thesis on how Rhode Island's economic engine responded to the Civil War, making weapons and uniforms for the Union cause. Zambarano argues that this wartime industrialization led to Rhode Island becoming the most urbanized, industrial state in the decades after the Civil War.

Chapter Two:

Biographical Sources

Adams, George W.

In Memoriam: Col. George William Adams. Providence: NP, 1883.

One of the finest battery commanders sent by Rhode Island, Adams was beloved by his men and served as a lieutenant in Battery B and captain of Battery G. He was thrice brevetted for gallantry in action and concocted the plan that led to seven Battery G soldiers being awarded the Medal of Honor on April 2, 1865. This booklet contains a sketch of this officer.

Bartlett, John Russell

Bartlett, John Russell. *Autobiography of John Russell Bartlett.* Edited by Jerry E. Mueller. Providence: John Carter Brown Library, 2006.

Rhode Island's longest serving Secretary of State, Bartlett played a very prominent role in Rhode Island politics in the Civil War. This detailed autobiography is compiled from Bartlett's papers housed at the John Carter Brown Library at Brown University. Bartlett provides a good view into his activities during the war, as well as his efforts to collect books, articles, and clippings relating to the war.

Burnside, Ambrose E.

Ballou, Daniel R. *The Military Services of Ambrose Everett Burnside in the Civil War, And their Value as an Asset of his Country and its History.* Providence: The Society, 1914.

A former lieutenant in the Twelfth Rhode Island, Ballou served a term as commander of the Department of Rhode Island, Grand Army of the Republic and was a very popular speaker in Rhode Island after the war. This sketch praises Burnside's actions at New Bern, in East Tennessee, and elsewhere, while negating his role at Antietam and Fredericksburg by placing the blame for his failures in those actions on others. Provides a good overview of Burnside's services during the war.

Burnside, Ambrose E. *The Burnside Expedition.* Providence: N. Bang Williams, 1882.

One of his only published works, this detailed overview of the Burnside Expedition was written by the general himself. He provides a superb overview of the strategy of the campaign and why he made certain decisions. Particularly useful in understanding how troops were selected to participate.

Burnside, Ambrose E. *Report of Committee and Papers.* Washington, D.C.: Government Printing Office, 1881.

Burnside's report and committee reports when he was trying to modernize the United States Army. Although not passed during his lifetime, many of these reforms were passed in the years after his 1881 death. Provides a fascinating insight into the cornerstone of the modern United States Army.

Cullen, Joseph P. "The Very Beau Ideal of a Soldier:" A Personality Profile of Ambrose E. Burnside." *Civil War Times Illustrated* (August 1977), 4-6: 7-9: 38-42: 44.

A brief biographical overview of Burnside's place in Civil War history.

Dedication of the Equestrian Statue of Major General Ambrose E. Burnside, July Fourth, Independence Day, 1887. Providence: R.I. Print Co., 1887.

Following his death in 1881, the Rhode Island General Assembly voted to erect a large equestrian statue of General Burnside in a park, now known as Burnside Park, in Providence. This dedication book from the event chronicles the building of the statue, memorial addresses given in Burnside's honor, and the highlights of the dedication ceremony. Of interest are listings of various Grand Army of the Republic Posts, dignitaries, as well as veteran groups that attended the dedication.

Edwards, Knight. "Burnside: A Rhode Island Hero." *Rhode Island History* Vol. 16, No. 1 (January 1957), 1-22.

A detailed, albeit brief biographical sketch of Burnside. Edwards, a Providence attorney attempts to place Burnside in his place in Rhode Island history. The cover includes a rare painting of Burnside drawn in 1852 while he was a Regular Army lieutenant stationed at Fort Adams.

Hess, Earl J. *The Knoxville Campaign: Burnside and Longstreet in East Tennessee.* Knoxville: University of Tennessee Press, 2013.

A detailed tactical campaign study of Burnside's role in the East Tennessee Campaign in the winter of 1863-1864. Provides an excellent treatment of Burnside's actions in the decisive Battle of Knoxville, as well as his role in liberating East Tennessee, the inhabitants of which largely supported the Union cause. This book paints Burnside as a very competent field commander.

Hull, Edward A. *Burnside Breach Loading Carbines, 1853-1866.* Lincoln: A. Mowbray, 1986.

Prior to the Civil War, Burnside had invented an ingeniously designed breach loading carbine. Unable to secure a large government contract, and heavily in debt, he sold the patent rights, never profiting off the weapon that carries his name. This book is the best source of material on the Burnside carbine. Heavily illustrated and well-researched, it provides information on the five different models of carbine, and the differences between each firearm.

Marvel, William. *Burnside.* Chapel Hill: University of North Carolina Press, 1991.

The only modern biography of Burnside, this book presents the beleaguered commander in a new light. Heavily researched entirely from primary sources, Marvel casts Burnside as a very competent and trusting Union commander who was let down time and again by the administration and his subordinates. Highly readable, this book is one of the best sources of material on this incredible soldier and statesman.

Memorial addresses on the Life and Character of Ambrose E. Burnside, (a Senator from Rhode Island) Delivered in the Senate and House of Representatives, Forty-seventh Congress, First Session, January 23, 1882. Washington, D.C.: Government Printing Office, 1882.

A compilation of addresses and resolutions passed in memory of Senator Burnside, who died in office in 1881. Very typical of the poetic language of the late nineteenth century.

Poore, Benjamin Perley. *The Life and Public Services of Ambrose E. Burnside, Soldier-Citizen-Statesman.* Providence: J.A. & R.A. Reid, 1882.

A comprehensive biography of Burnside, published shortly after his death, this book provides a very good view into Rhode Island's most famous Civil War soldier. Poore covers Burnside's early life in Indiana, his Civil War service, and his political career as governor and senator from Rhode Island. Typical of nineteenth century biographies, this one praises Burnside's victories at New Bern and in East Tennessee, while down playing his role at Fredericksburg and the Crater in 1864.

Sauers, Richard A. *"A Succession of Honorable Victories:" The Burnside Expedition in North Carolina.* Dayton: Morningside House, 1996.

In the winter and spring of 1862, Burnside led an expedition to the Outer Banks of North Carolina that captured much of the Carolina coast for the Union, including the city of New Bern. The majority of troops in the Burnside Expedition were New Englanders; these troops would later form the nucleus of the Ninth Corps. A very detailed account of the campaign filled with primary sources and maps. Provides a good understanding of Burnside as a general officer.

Tenney, Craig D. "Major General A. E. Burnside and the First Amendment: A Case Study of Civil War Freedom of Expression." Ph. D. Dissertation, Indiana University, 1977.

A thorough case study of Burnside's 1863 arrest and banishment of Clement Vallandigham of Ohio. The leader of the Copperhead movement, and a former Congressman, Vallandigham was arrested after speaking out against the Lincoln administration. This is an excellent treatment of this controversial event.

Thomas, Donna. "Ambrose E. Burnside and Army Reform, 1850-1881." *Rhode Island History* Vol. 37, No. 1 (February 1978), 3-14.

A thoroughly researched article that narrates Burnside's efforts, as a United States senator to reform the United States Army based on his own experiences as an officer. Burnside attempted to raise the pay of enlisted men and expand the role of black troops in the army, as well as create a retirement program for officers and enlisted men. Although revolutionary at the time, few of these reforms were initiated during Burnside's time in the Senate.

Tucker, Phillip Thomas. *Burnside's Bridge: The Climactic Struggle of the 2nd and 20th Georgia at Antietam Creek.* Mechanicsburg: Stackpole Books, 2011.

The most detailed study regarding the attack on the Rohrbach Bridge at Antietam. After the battle, the bridge, which still stands over Antietam Creek, and is an iconic remnant of the fight there was renamed Burnside Bridge.

Wahlde, Urban C. "Ambrose Burnside and the Ninth Corps: Four Photographs from a Moment of Glory." *Rhode Island History* Vol. 66, No. 1 (Winter/Spring 2008), 23-32.

An interesting article about the development of the Ninth Corps badge in the spring of 1864. Provides in-depth information on the state of Burnside and the Ninth Corps shortly before the start of the Overland Campaign, as well as several interesting photographs of Burnside.

Woodbury, Augustus. *Ambrose Everett Burnside.* Providence: N. Bang Williams, 1882.

Woodbury's personal reminiscences of Burnside, as presented in a paper to the Soldiers and Sailors Historical Society.

Woodbury, Augustus. *Major General Ambrose E. Burnside and the Ninth Army Corps: A Narrative of Campaigns in North Carolina, Maryland, Virginia, Ohio, Kentucky, Mississippi, and Tennessee, During the War for the Preservation of the Union.* Providence: Sidney S. Rider, 1867.

Commanded by Burnside for most of the war, and including Rhode Island regiments such as the Fourth, Fifth, Seventh, and Twelfth Regiments, the Ninth Corps traveled further and fought in more engagements than any other Union corps. This book is a comprehensive history of the Ninth Corps. Woodbury details the raising of the corps for the Burnside Expedition and its subsequent campaigns in the Eastern and Western Theatres. Particular attention is paid to the Rhode Island regiments in the corps. Also included is a full list of staff officers, officers of the corps that died in the war, as well as regiments that served in the Ninth Corps. A very informative history.

Woodbury, Augustus. *The Soldier, Senator, Man: An Address Delivered at the Funeral of Ambrose Everett Burnside, in Providence, R.I., September 16, 1881*. Providence: E.L. Freeman and Co, 1884.

Given at the funeral of General Burnside in 1881, this is Woodbury's fitting testimonial to Burnside's service to the people of Rhode Island.

Duffie, Alfred N.

Bliss, George N. *Duffie and the Monument to His Memory*. Providence: The Society, 1890.

This is a biographical sketch of Colonel Duffie and his role in leading the First Rhode Island Cavalry. Bliss does a good job in providing details regarding his role in the Civil War. Duffie's background is often mistaken, and Bliss repeats these details here. Duffie was not a graduate of the French military academy. Rather he had deserted the French Army and made his way to America, where marrying into a prominent family, he earned his commissions in the Union forces through patronage and his own battlefield prowess. Despite lying about his past, Duffie was a competent Federal cavalry commander. Also included in this work is the memorial dedicated to Duffie's memory in North Burial Ground in Providence; the general himself is buried on Staten Island.

Shepard, James C. "Alfred N. Duffie and the First Rhode Island Cavalry in the American Civil War." M.A. Thesis, Louisiana State University, 1972.

An above average master's thesis that provides detailed information regarding Duffie's service as a commander at the company, regimental, and brigade level during the Civil War, focusing in large part on his command of the First Rhode Island

Cavalry and his training to turn the regiment into a very competent fighting force after taking command in the summer of 1862.

Greene, George Sears

In Memoriam, George Sears Greene: Brevet Major-General, United States Volunteers, 1801-1899. Albany: New York Monuments Commission, 1909.

A native of Warwick, Greene was a West Pointer who had moved to New York before the war. At age sixty he became colonel of the Sixtieth New York and later became a general. He served with distinction at Cedar Mountain and Antietam, but is best remembered for his defense of Culp's Hill at Gettysburg. Greene lived to be ninety-eight and is buried in Warwick. In 1909 a statue to his memory was erected on Culp's Hill by the State of New York.

Ethier, Eric. "George Sears Greene: Gettysburg's Other Second-Day Hero." *Rhode Island History* Vol. 53, No. 2 (May 1995), 59-68.

A detailed view of Greene's actions on Culp's Hill at Gettysburg on the night of July 2-3, 1863.

Hawkins, Rush C.

Stillwell, Margaret Bingham. *Librarians are Human: Memories In and Out of the Rare-Book World 1907-1970.* Boston: Colonial Society of Massachusetts, 1973.

Colonel Rush C. Hawkins served in the Civil War as commander of the Ninth New York, a Zouave regiment he recruited that fought with the Ninth Corps in the Burnside Expedition and at Antietam. He also married into the Brown family of Providence. Stillwell served as the private librarian to Hawkins during his time building a massive private collection of art and books. The book is exceptionally well written and contains much information on Hawkins. The Ann Mary Brown Memorial at Brown University contains a Civil War museum holding Hawkins' military collections and paintings; he and his wife are also interred in a crypt in the back of the building.

Hay, John

The Life and Works of John Hay 1838-1905: A Commemorative Catalogue of the Exhibition Shown at the John Hay Library of Brown University in Honor of the Centennial of his Graduation at the Commencement of 1858. Providence: Brown University, 1961.

One of Brown's most famous alumni, John Hay went on to serve as private secretary to President Lincoln and later gave his name to Brown's Special Collections Library. This book is a guide to Hay manuscripts at the Hay Library. Among the works quoted in this book are several of Hay's journal extracts from 1861 when he visited the First Rhode Island Detached Militia in camp at Washington and interacted with several friends he had made at Brown.

Lincoln, Abraham

Williams, Frank J. "A Candidate Speaks in Rhode Island: Abraham Lincoln Visits Providence and Woonsocket, 1860." *Rhode Island History* Vol. 51, No. 4 (November 1993), 107-120.

In the spring of 1860, while campaigning for president, Abraham Lincoln made two campaign stops in Rhode Island, one in Providence and one in Woonsocket where he delivered a version of his famed Cooper Union speech. Williams, a nationally recognized Lincoln scholar and former chief justice of the Rhode Island Supreme Court chronicles Lincoln's visit to Rhode Island and the reaction of Rhode Islanders to his speeches.

Holzer, Harold. "Lincoln and Lincolniana." *Books at Brown* Vol. XXXI-XXXII (1984-1985)

The John Hay Library at Brown University is home to the McLellan Lincoln Collection, one of the largest Lincoln research collections in the United States, as well as the papers of Lincoln's private secretary John Hay. This special addition of *Books at Brown* provides an in-depth look into the creation of the collection and the materials available within it.

Rogers, Horatio

Field, Edward. *Memorial of Horatio Rogers, one of the record commissioners of the City of Providence, died November 12, 1904.* Providence: Snow & Farnum, 1904.

Rogers served in the Civil War in the Third Rhode Island Heavy Artillery and as colonel, led the Second Rhode Island Volunteers at Chancellorsville and Gettysburg. After the war, he became attorney general of Rhode Island and was an associate justice on the Rhode Island Supreme Court. He was also a prolific author, book collector, and researcher who chaired a committee that published the early records of Providence. This book is a memorial of his lifetime achievements.

Rodman, Isaac Peace

Gough, Robert E. *South Kingstown's Own: A Biographical Sketch of Isaac Peace Rodman, brigadier general.* Kingston: University of Rhode Island, 2011.

A very good biographical sketch of General Isaac Peace Rodman. A native of South Kingstown, Rodman was a prominent mill owner before the war who recruited a company for the Second Rhode Island where he served as captain. Appointed colonel of the Fourth Rhode Island he won a general's star for heroism at the Battle of New Bern. He was mortally wounded at Antietam and became the highest ranked Rhode Island officer to die in the Civil War. Contrary to popular belief, he was Baptist, not a Quaker.

Sprague, William

Hoffman, Charles and Tess Hoffman. *Brotherly Love: Murder and the Politics of Prejudice in Nineteenth-Century Rhode Island.* Amherst: University of Massachusetts Press, 1993.

Governor Sprague's father, Amasa, a very prominent and wealthy textile manufacturer was killed in Cranston in 1843. Three local Irishmen were arrested for the crime, and one, John Gordon was the last man put to death in Rhode Island. The authors speculate that it was actually Amasa's brother, Senator William Sprague who killed his brother to gain control of the company. A fascinating view into life in nineteenth century Rhode Island, and how this event affected the future "war governor."

Huston, James L. "The Threat of Radicalism: Seward's Candidacy and the Rhode Island Gubernatorial Election of 1860." *Rhode Island History* Vol. 41, No. 3 (August 1982), 87-99.

A very interesting article about the 1860 gubernatorial election in Rhode Island in which William Sprague, originally a Democrat overcame Seth Padelford who was running on the Republican platform. Sprague won the election by a margin of two to one and then became a Republican! Huston also offers details about the origins of the Republican Party in Rhode Island.

Lamphier, Peg A. *Kate Chase and William Sprague: Politics and Gender in a Civil War Marriage.* Lincoln: University of Nebraska Press, 2003.

An interesting volume, this is the best study for the tumultuous relationship between Senator William Sprague and his wife Kate. Deeply researched, and well-written, it shows that Kate was much more involved in political affairs of the time than previously thought. The book also provides detailed insight into Rhode Island politics of the Civil War era, as well as the sociological aspects of marriage in the Civil War era.

Oller, John. *American Queen: The Rise and Fall of Kate Chase Sprague, Civil War "Belle of the North" and Gilded Age Woman of Scandal.* New York: Da Capo Press, 2014.

Another book about the scandal filled marriage of William and Kate Sprague.

Sprague, William. *The Tax Bill. Speech of William Sprague in the Senate of the United States April 8, 1869.* Washington, D.C.: Government Printing Office, 1869.

Although he took the Senate floor to debate a tax bill, Senator Sprague in a drunken tirade attacked Ambrose Burnside and the men of the First Rhode Island Detached Militia, calling them cowards and misfits. This led to a large reversal of public opinion against Sprague, especially by the veterans of Rhode Island. In the next senatorial election, Burnside replaced Sprague in the United States Senate; Sprague never again held elected office in Rhode Island.

Stevens, Isaac Ingalls

Stevens, Hazard. *Life of Isaac Ingalls Stevens.* New York: Houghton Mifflin, 1901.

Although born in Massachusetts, General Isaac Ingalls Stevens is indelibly connected to Rhode Island. He served at Fort Adams before the war and married into a prominent Newport family. Stevens was the first governor of the Washington Territory and was killed in action at Chantilly, Virginia on September 1, 1862. He is buried in Island Cemetery in Newport. His son, Hazard, a native of Newport, is buried beside him, served on his staff, and earned the Medal of Honor.

Wheaton, Frank

Report of Commission to erect a monument in Arlington Cemetery, Virginia to the memory of the late Major-

General Frank Wheaton Made at the January session 1905. Providence: E.L. Freeman & Sons, 1905.

A native of Providence, Frank Wheaton was a Regular Army officer who became the second colonel of the Second Rhode Island. He later became a brigadier and brevet major general, g`lqserving as a very competent brigade and division commander in the Sixth Corps. This report details Rhode Island efforts to erect a monument in his memory at Arlington National Cemetery.

Chapter Three:

Rhode Island Militia Sources

Brown, Howard F. and Roberta Mudge Humble. *The Historic Armories of Rhode Island.* Pawtucket: Globe Print Co., 2000.

A fantastic look at the many historical armories located throughout Rhode Island, many of which were built in the years after the Dorr Rebellion and became recruiting centers during the Civil War. Highly illustrated, and well researched, this is a great resource for information on the Rhode Island Militia. Brown served as an officer in World War II and Korea, while Humble, who was heavily involved in the restoration of the Westerly Armory was an English professor.

DeSimone, Russell J. and Daniel C. Schofield. *The Broadsides of the Dorr Rebellion.* Providence: Rhode Island Supreme Court Historical Society, 1992.

Published to commemorate the sesquicentennial of the Dorr Rebellion, this book includes many illustrations from the period and is very useful to illustrate the dress and actions of the Rhode Island Militia in the antebellum era.

Dyer, Elisha Sr. "Rhode Island in 1842." *The Narragansett Historical Register: Volume 6.* Pp. 145-197.

The adjutant general was the senior officer of the Rhode Island Militia, and during the Civil War was the office that mustered and equipped volunteers for Federal service. This informative essay was written by Elisha Dyer Sr., who went on to serve as governor of Rhode Island and in the Civil War as a captain in the Tenth Rhode Island. This sketch provides an in-depth look into the workings of the department during the Dorr Rebellion and Dyer's efforts to modernize the adjutant general's office.

Ernst, Howard R. "A Call to Arms: Thomas Wilson Dorr's
    Forceful Effort to Implement the People's Constitution."
    Rhode Island History Vol. 66, No. 3 (Fall 2008), 59-80.

The most detailed account of Dorr's May 1842 attempt to capture the Providence arsenal in his attempt to implement the People's Government of Rhode Island. Deeply researched and highly illustrated. This article provides an excellent view into the antebellum activities of the Rhode Island Militia.

*History of the Organization of the First Light Infantry Veteran
    Association of Providence, R.I.* Providence: NP, 1870.

A detailed history and roster of members of the First Light Infantry of Providence. During the Civil War, the First Light Infantry served as Companies C and D of the First Rhode Island Detached Militia.

Lancaster, Jane. "The Battle of Chepachet: An Eyewitness
    Account." *Rhode Island History* Vol. 62, No. 1
    (Winter/Spring 2004), 17-24.

An exceptionally well written and edited account of the only "battle" of the Dorr Rebellion, written by a member of the Providence Marine Corps of Artillery which took part in the action at Chepachet in June 1842. Very useful in understanding the Providence Marine Corps of Artillery in the years before the Civil War.

Memorial of William Waterman Brown. Providence: First Light
    Infantry Veteran Association, 1887.

Colonel William Waterman Brown was one of the most experienced soldiers in Rhode Island at the start of the Civil War. He served for decades in the First Light Infantry of Providence. He was involved in the 1831 Snow Town Riot in Providence, and led the forces of the Law & Order Party during the 1842 engagement at Acotes Hill during the Dorr Rebellion. He served in the Civil

War as a captain in the First Rhode Island Detached Militia and spent the rest of the war at home recruiting and drilling men. This interesting book includes details on his life, as well as the impressive monument erected to his memory in Swan Point Cemetery.

McAfee, Michael J. "The First Light Infantry of Providence, Rhode Island." *Military Images* Vol. 14, No. 3 (November/December 1992), 28-29.

An analysis of the pre-war uniforms of the First Light Infantry which composed bearskin helmet, red coat, and sky-blue trousers.

Mowbray, E. Andrew and Andrew W. Young. "Rhode Island Militia Flags." *Military Collector and Historian* Vol. 19, No. 2 (Summer 1967), special insert.

A special insert into this issue of *Military Collector,* this full color, four page spread features full color images of many early Rhode Island Militia flags. Detailed photographs which show the evolution of Rhode Island Militia colors.

Mowry, Arthur May. *The Dorr War: or the Constitutional Struggle in Rhode Island.* Providence: Preston & Rounds, 1901.

The first and perhaps best scholarly book ever published on the Dorr Rebellion, this book, unlike many others focuses on the military aspects of the Dorr Rebellion. Heavily illustrated with engravings of military actions and maps, Mowry's book provides a crucial understanding of the Rhode Island Militia units that took part in the Dorr Rebellion and later responded to events early in the Civil War.

Richards, J.J. *Rhode Island's Early Defenders and Their Successors.* East Greenwich: Rhode Island Pendulum, 1937.

The most important source for information on the history of the Rhode Island Militia, Richards, the adjutant general of the state before World War II produced this impressive history, providing detailed information regarding the various units of the Rhode Island Militia from the Revolution through World War I. Using this book, one can trace the lineage of a particular unit. Especially helpful in identifying Rhode Island Militia units in service during the Dorr Rebellion and the Civil War.

Schroder, Walter K. *The Artillery Company of Newport (A Pictorial History)*. Berwyn Heights, MD: Heritage Books, 2014.

The Artillery Company of Newport, chartered in 1741 is the oldest chartered unit still in service in the Rhode Island Militia, and is today a reenacting organization, while also preserving a vast collection of militaria in their armory in Newport. This book is a pictorial study of the Newport Artillery and includes many rare photographs of the unit.

Swan, James C. "The Newport Artillery in 1842, Federal Hill and Chepachet." *The Narragansett Historical Register: Volume 7*. Pp. 24-34.

A gripping account of the role the Artillery Company of Newport played in the Dorr Rebellion.

Todd, Frederick P. *American Military Equipage, 1851-1872: A Description by Word and Picture of what the American Soldier, Sailor, and Marine of these years wore and carried, with an emphasis on the American Civil War.* New York: Scribner, 1980. Pp. 1149-1161.

A very detailed account of the uniforms, weapons, and equipage worn by each Rhode Island unit during the Civil War era. Of particular note are the detailed descriptions of the pre-war militia uniforms for units such as the Pawtucket Light Guard, Westerly Rifles, and Kentish Guards, which later formed part of the early group of Rhode Island Volunteers. The chapter on Rhode Island is highly illustrated.

Wells, Cyril L.D. *Outline History of the 243rd Coast Artillery (HD)*. East Greenwich: The Greenwich Press, 1928.

A regiment that is still active in the Rhode Island National Guard, the 243rd has an illustrious history and was composed, before World War II of companies from throughout Rhode Island. This sketch of the regiment provides the lineage of each company, most of which could trace their history back to units that fought in the Civil War.

Chapter Four:

Infantry Sources

First Rhode Island Detached Militia

Archambault, Alan H. "The First Regiment Rhode Island Detached Militia, 1861." *Military Collector and Historian* Vol. 53, No. 3 (Fall 2001), 98-109.

The First Rhode Island wore a unique uniform and went to war with a combination of militia equipment when they mustered in April 1861. In this very detailed article, Archambault, a native of Warwick, and a Rhode Island College graduate who later went on to become chief of the U.S. Army museum service, as well as being a noted artist, analyzes the uniforms worn by the different companies of the regiment. The article is highly illustrated and includes many sketches by Archambault.

Bartlett, Sara. "Kady Brownell, a Rhode Island Legend." *Minerva: Quarterly Report on Women and the Military* (Summer 2001), 39-58.

Kady Brownell is a widely known Rhode Island Civil War figure who served in the honorary role as the "Regimental Daughter" for the First Rhode Island Detached Militia and Fifth Rhode Island Heavy Artillery. Living in Providence before the war, she followed her husband Robert to war who served in both units. Brownell became a bit of a celebrity after the war due to her alleged wartime exploits carrying the colors of the First Rhode Island at Bull Run and toured the country. This article attempts to separate the facts from the many myths that have sprung up around Brownell's service.

Clarke, Charles H. *History of Company F, 1st Regiment, R.I. Volunteers, During the Spring and Summer of 1861.* Newport: B.W. Pearce, Printer, 1891.

A detailed account of Newport's response to the Civil War through the service of the Artillery Company of Newport, which became Company F of the First Rhode Island Detached Militia. Provides an excellent account of the early morning action at Bull Run.

Grefe, C. Morgan. "Sourcing a Rhode Island Legend." *Rhode Island History* Vol.70, No. 1 (Winter Spring 2012), 31-43.

Another article about Kady Brownell, this piece by the director of the Rhode Island Historical Society provides insight into the Brownell materials within the society collections. Grefe focuses on Brownell's actions after the war and how she became a Rhode Island legend. While present on the field with her husband, Kady did not perform many of the deeds she later claimed to have done.

Nosworthy, Brent. *Roll Call to Destiny: The Soldier's Eye View of Civil War Battles.* New York: Basic Books, 2008. Pp. 33-83.

A Providence based scholar who has authored numerous works on military tactics, this book describes Civil War combat across different terrain features and how that terrain, weapons, and tactics afflicted the outcome of the battle. Nosworthy writes a detailed chapter of the opening action at Bull Run as the First and Second Rhode Island Regiments fought a battle in the open on Matthew's Hill against a brigade of troops from Georgia and Alabama. Very detailed and highly researched.

A Service in Memory of the Reverend Augustus Woodbury, D.D., held in the Westminster Congregational Church, Providence, R.I., Sunday, December 15, 1895. Providence: Westminster Congregational Society, 1895.

The sermon preached at the funeral of Augustus Woodbury, it recalls his service in the Civil War and his writings about Rhode Island's Civil War soldiers.

Smith, George B. "Formation and Service of the First Regiment Rhode Island Detached Militia." *Bulletin of the Newport Historical Society* No. 58 (July 1926), 14-29.

An interesting sketch of the First Rhode Island, written by an aged veteran who served in Company F from Newport. Provides some interesting details regarding Smith's service at Bull Run and how Newport responded to the war.

Sturtevant, Mary Clark. *Thomas March Clark: Fifth Bishop of Rhode Island, A Memoir.* Milwaukee: Morehouse Publishing Co., 1927. Pp. 86-103.

The Episcopal Bishop of Rhode Island, Clark spent several weeks at Camp Sprague, the headquarters of Rhode Island troops in Washington shortly before the First Battle of Bull Run in June 1861. His letters provide details regarding the camp life of the Rhode Islanders, as well as their religious activities. The camp of the Second Rhode Island was named Camp Clark in his honor.

Warren, Richard. *Federal Data Series: 1st Rhode Island Detached Militia, 2nd Rhode Island Volunteer Infantry, 1st and 2nd Rhode Island Batteries 1861.* Fife, Scotland: Confederate Historical Society, 1987.

Published in Scotland by a Civil War historical society, this booklet is a surprisingly good analysis of the uniforms worn by the First and Second Rhode Island early in the war. While comparable to Archambault's article above, this one includes details of the uniforms of the various militia groups comprising the First Rhode Island. Difficult to find in the United States, this booklet is very informative. Heavily illustrated with drawings by the author.

Woodbury, Augustus. *The Memory of the First Battle: A Discourse Preached in Westminster Church, Providence, R.I. on the 28th Anniversary of the Battle of Bull Run, July 21, 1889, Before the Veteran Associations of the First and Second Rhode Island Regiments and Their Batteries.* Providence: E.L. Freeman, 1889.

A thorough treatment of Bull Run, Woodbury recalls the battle nearly thirty years later in this interesting discourse. Also includes information regarding the members of the First who reenlisted in other units. Of the 1,200 men who served in the First Rhode Island, 850 went on to serve in other regiments in Rhode Island and elsewhere during the war.

Woodbury, Augustus. *A Narrative of the Campaign of the First Rhode Island Regiment, in the Spring and Summer of 1861.* Providence: Sidney S. Rider, 1862.

As stated in the introduction, this book was the very first regimental history to be published about a Civil War unit. Highly detailed, Woodbury's account set the standard by which all future histories would be written. This book chronicles Rhode Island's response to the Civil War in April 1861, as well as the First's actions at Bull Run. Woodbury includes biographical sketches of the fallen members of the regiment, as well as a list of those who had reenlisted in other units. An excellent account of the First Rhode Island.

Woodbury, Augustus. *The Uprising of 1861: The Illustration of True Patriotism: A Sermon preached in Providence, R.I. July 21, 1895, before the Veteran Associations of the First and Second Rhode Island Regiments and Batteries.* Providence: Providence Press, 1895.

Another of Woodbury's many writings on the early history of Rhode Island and the Civil War. This booklet is particularly interesting in Woodbury's descriptions of events in Providence following the firing on Fort Sumter and the initial surge of volunteers for the First and Second Rhode Island Regiments.

Second Rhode Island Volunteers

Archambault, Alan G. "2nd Rhode Island Volunteer Infantry, 1861-1865." *Military Collector & Historian* Vol. 43, No. 1 (Spring 1991), 32-35.

An interesting series of sketches and accompanying text on how the uniforms of the Second Rhode Island Volunteers evolved during their four years of service in the Army of the Potomac.

Banks, John. "On the Eve of First Blood: Rhode Islander's Before First Bull Run." *Military Images* Vol. 35, No. 1 (Winter 2017), 18-20.

A popular New England Civil War blogger, John Banks, in this photographical analysis, analyzes a very interesting collection of photographs of the Second Rhode Island Volunteers in the collection of the Providence Public Library. Taken at "Bush Camp" on the march to Bull Run in 1861, these rare images show the Second Rhode Island shortly before the first major battle of the war. The images are very candid and show the men as they appear in the field on campaign. Banks writes about the context of the photos and the fates of the men in the images.

Caldwell, Samuel L. *A Sermon Preached in the First Baptist Meeting-House, Providence, Sunday morning, June 9, 1861, before the Second Regiment Rhode Island Volunteers.* Providence: Knowles, Anthony & Co., 1861.

Before leaving Rhode Island for the front, the men of the Second Rhode Island assembled in the First Baptist Meeting House in Providence to hear a riveting speech by the minister about the righteousness of their cause and that God was on the side of the Union. An interesting early war sermon.

Crossley, William J. *Extracts from my Diary, and From my Experiences while Boarding with Jefferson Davis in three of his Notorious Hotels, in Richmond, Va., Tuscaloosa,*

Ala., and Salisbury, N.C., from July 1861 to June 1862. Providence: The Society, 1903.

Crossley, a sergeant in the Second Rhode Island was wounded at Bull Run and captured by the Confederates. His narrative provides excellent information regarding the treatment of Union wounded after the battle, as well as an eye-witness account to the deaths of Colonel Slocum and Major Ballou. It is interesting to compare his writings about the treatment of Union prisoners of war in the early stages of the war to those held captive as the war progressed. A very detailed account.

Grandchamp, Robert. "O Sarah!: Did Sullivan Ballou's famed letter come from another's pen?" *America's Civil War* (November 2017), 31-35.

A highly controversial article, in this piece, Grandchamp analyzes the history of the famed July 14, 1861 letter attributed to Major Sullivan Ballou and read during Ken Burns' Civil War series in 1991. Through in-depth analysis, Grandchamp, as well as two independent analysts conclude that Major Ballou was not the author of the letter. Grandchamp concludes the missive was actually written by Horatio Rogers, a close friend of Ballou as a memorial for his fallen friend.

Grandchamp, Robert. "The Second Rhode Island Volunteers in the Gettysburg Campaign." *Gettysburg Magazine* 42 (January 2010), 71-82.

The Second Rhode Island Volunteers played an interesting role in the Gettysburg Campaign. Although not heavily engaged in the battle, the regiment completed a grueling thirty-five mile forced march on July 2, 1863 to arrive on the field. Afterwards they were engaged in long range firefight and took part in a skirmish during Lee's retreat back to Virginia. Article is heavily noted and illustrated.

Henshaw, Ray and Glenn W. LaFantaise. "Letters Home: Sergeant Charles E. Perkins in Virginia, 1862." *Rhode Island History* Vol. 39, No. 4 (November 1980), 106-131.

Written largely from the Virginia Peninsula in the summer of 1862, Perkins' letters provide interesting details of the Second Rhode Island's role in the campaign. Perkins is adamant in his letters he was fighting to only restore the Union and not to end slavery. Also included are detailed letters regarding Antietam and Fredericksburg. Perkins survived the war and rose to captain. His original letters are at the Rhode Island Historical Society in Providence.

Jones, Evan C. "The Macabre Fate of Sullivan Ballou." *America's Civil War* (November 2004), 30-37.

After he was mortally wounded and died following the Battle of Bull Run, the remains of Major Sullivan Ballou were exhumed by a Georgia regiment and desecrated; the Georgians apparently wanting revenge on Rhode Islanders for the destruction of a brother regiment at Bull Run. This fascinating article chronicles what happened to Ballou after he died, as well as Governor William Sprague's efforts to recover his and the other remains of Rhode Islanders from Bull Run.

Martin, Jacob H. *The Campaign Life of Lt. Col. Henry Harrison Young: Aid-De-Camp to General Sheridan and Chief of His Scouts.* Providence: Sidney S. Rider, 1882.

Young served as the major of the Second Rhode Island Volunteers during the latter part of the Civil War. He is most known however as being commander of Sheridan's Scouts, a group of Union soldiers who operated in the Shenandoah Valley in 1864-1865. Dressed in Confederate clothing, they provided vital intelligence to General Sheridan. This book provides some interesting evidence of Young's career and quotes liberally from his letters, as well as anecdotes of his service from both Union and Confederate soldiers. Young was killed in Mexico in 1866 while scouting and raising troops to fight Maximillian. He body was never recovered.

Peck, George B. *Reminiscences of the War of the Rebellion.* Providence: Providence Press, 1884.

A student at Brown University for most of the conflict, Peck joined the war early in 1865 as a lieutenant in the Second Rhode Island. He took part in the storming of Petersburg and the Battle of Sailor's Creek where he was wounded. After the war, Peck became a physician in Providence and was heavily involved in veteran's affairs and the Grand Army of the Republic. This booklet contains his reminiscences of life on the Petersburg siege line and the problems often faced among Union troops in the trenches. Peck later expanded on his memoirs in two narratives for the Soldiers and Sailors Historical Society.

Peck, George B. *A Recruit Before Petersburg.* Providence: N. Bang Williams, 1880.

A highly detailed account of Peck's life on the Petersburg siege line late in the war. Peck wrote about the horrors of trench warfare with the naiveté of a soldier who had never seen combat before. Provides a good view of the relationship between veteran soldiers and new recruits. Peck participated in the Appomattox Campaign and writes about his wounding at Sailor's Creek, three days before the war ended.

Peck, George B. *Camp and Hospital.* Providence: The Society, 1884.

Another sketch by Peck, this narrative is divided into two parts. The first part contends with Peck's duties at a conscript camp near New Haven Connecticut in the winter of 1865 as he recruits and drills men for what eventually became Company G of the Second Rhode Island. The second part of his work picks up where *A Recruit Before Petersburg* left off and details his recovery after being wounded at Sailor's Creek. Taken together these two sketches are a highly detailed look into the final campaigns of the Second Rhode Island.

Rhodes, Elisha Hunt, and Robert Hunt Rhodes. *All for the Union: A History of the 2nd Rhode Island Volunteer Infantry in the War of the Great Rebellion As Told by the Diary and Letters of Elisha Hunt Rhodes, Who Enlisted As a Private in '61 and Rose to the Command of His Regiment.* Lincoln, RI: A. Mowbray, 1985.

Made famous by Ken Burns in his 1990 Civil War series, Rhodes, who rose from private to colonel of the Second Rhode Island, became the spokesman for the common Union soldier in the series. After the war, Rhodes rewrote his memoirs using his field diary and letters sent home to Cranston. The originals of these materials are at the Rhode Island Historical Society. Rhodes' narrative is clear, well written, and detailed. He saw service in all the major battles of the Army of the Potomac and lived to tell the story. A remarkable account of the war, and the most widely read book written by a Rhode Island soldier; it was reissued in paperback in 1992 by Random House.

Rhodes, Elisa Hunt. *The First Campaign of the Second Rhode Island Volunteers.* Providence: Sidney S. Rider, 1878.

This was the first published pamphlet by the Soldiers and Sailors Historical Society. In this sketch, Rhodes narrates the raising and mustering of the Second Rhode Island. He provides a good overview of the Second at Bull Run; Rhodes assisted Colonel Slocum after he was mortally wounded. Much of this material was later incorporated in *All For the Union.*

Rhodes, Elisha Hunt. *The Second Rhode Island Volunteers at the Siege of Petersburg, Virginia.* Providence: The Society, 1915.

This is the final publication of the Rhode Island Soldiers and Sailors Historical Society and was published two years before Rhodes' death. As with the above work, a large part of this sketch was later republished in *All For the Union.* In his final work, Rhodes detailed the role of the Second Rhode Island at Petersburg, their life in the trenches, and the participation of the regiment in the April 2, 1865 assault that broke Lee's lines.

Roelker, William Greene. "Civil War Letters of William Ames." *Rhode Island Historical Society Collections* Vol. 33, No. 4 (October 1940), 73-92.

Roelker, William Greene. "Civil War Letters of William Ames." *Rhode Island Historical Society Collections* Vol. 34, No. 1 (January 1941), 5-24.

Originally a lieutenant in Company D of the Second Rhode Island, Ames later became colonel of the Third Rhode Island Heavy Artillery. These two articles about Ames' service reflect the first few months of the war. Ames chronicles the raising of the Second Rhode Island, as well as life at Camp Clark in Washington in the days before Bull Run. His letters give one of the best views of the Second at the battle; Ames is highly critical of the performance of some of the officers in the regiment and this adds to these letters historical value.

Rogers, Horatio. *Personal Experiences of the Chancellorsville Campaign.* Providence: N. Bang Williams, 1881.

Written by the commander of the Second Rhode Island during the 1863 campaigns, Rogers writes one of the best narratives published by the Soldiers and Sailors Historical Society. This sketch narrates Rogers' acceptance into the regiment as an outsider, having been transferred from the Third Rhode Island. He writes in great detail about the Second Rhode Island's role at the storming of Mayre's Heights on May 3, 1863 and their later participation the same day at Salem's Church. Of great note is Rogers writing how tactics were often forgotten in combat as officers had to improvise in the field. A very important work.

Rolston, Les. *Long Time Gone: Neighbors Divided by Civil War.* Tampa: Mariner Publishing, 2009.

In the 1840s, Elisha Hunt Rhodes and James Rhodes Sheldon were neighbors growing up together in Pawtuxet village. In the 1850s, Sheldon moved with his family to Georgia. He joined the Fiftieth Georgia Regiment in the Civil War, while Rhodes served in the Second Rhode Island. A well-researched local history book, this volume provides insight into the Rhode Island experience of brother against brother.

Spicer, William A. *Colonel Henry H. Young in the Civil War: Sheridan's Chief of Scouts, A noted Rhode Island fighter.* Providence: E.A. Johnson & Co., 1910.

In 1910, the State of Rhode Island erected a monument to Young's honor in Burnside Park in Providence. Called "The Scout," the monument, which is a life size statue of Young honors his service. This booklet provides a brief biography and story of the monument.

Weinert, Richard P. "The South had Mosby; The Union: Maj. Henry Young." *Civil War Times Illustrated* (April 1964), 39-42.

A good article about Major Young's spy work in the Shenandoah Valley in the summer and fall of 1864, focusing on Young's battles against Major Harry Gilmore's Confederate cavalry.

Woodbury, Augustus. *The Second Rhode Island Regiment: A Narrative of Military Operations in Which the Regiment Was Engaged from the Beginning to the End of the War for the Union.* Providence: Valpey, Angell, and Co, 1875.

Woodbury's second published regimental history, this volume is a detailed history of the Second Rhode Island and its service in all the actions of the Army of the Potomac from Bull Run to Appomattox. Based on the memoirs and letters of several veterans, this stout volume covers the history of this gallant regiment. Of utmost importance are detailed biographical sketches of every soldier in the regiment who lost his life while serving in the Second Rhode Island.

Young, Robin. *For Love & Liberty: The Untold Civil War Story of Major Sullivan Ballou & His Famous Love Letter.* New York: Thunder's Mouth Press, 2005.

This book is one of the worst written about Rhode Island and the Civil War. Written as a biography of Major Ballou, this book bogs down in the cultural aspects of the mid-nineteenth century and provides as much information on marriage, children, the practice of law, and education, as it does on Ballou. Poorly written, this book does not have much value.

Fourth Rhode Island Volunteers

Allen, George H. *Forty-Six Months with the Fourth R.I. Volunteers, in the War of 1861 to 1865 Comprising a History of Its Marches, Battles, and Camp Life. Compiled from Journals Kept While on Duty in the Field and Camp, by Corp. Geo. H. Allen.* Providence: J.A. & R.A. Reid, 1887.

Originally published as his memoirs, this book was later adopted by the Fourth Rhode Island as their official regimental history. A corporal from Providence, Allen kept a meticulous journal during the war. This volume provides one of the best accounts of the Battle of New Bern, as well as the Fourth's actions at Antietam and the Crater at Petersburg. Highly readable, Allen wrote clearly and with a sense of preserving the deeds of his regiment for posterity. The book also provides details regarding the bitter feud between the Fourth and Seventh Rhode Island Regiments.

Chartrand, Rene. "O Canada!: Canada's National Anthem: Composed by Calixa Lavallee, 4th Rhode Island Regiment, 1861-1862." *Military Collector and Historian* Vol. 53, No. 3 (Fall 2001), 110.

A brief but interesting article regarding the unique uniform worn by the band of the Fourth Rhode Island during their service; the band was mustered out shortly after Antietam.

Civil War Letters of Hugh McInnes. Parsons, WV: McClain Publishing, 1981.

McInnes was from Richmond and served as a sergeant in Company A of the Fourth Rhode Island; he lost an arm at the Battle of the Crater, July 30, 1864. These are above average soldier's letters with McInnes frequently writing home about life in the South. Of particular importance are letters written about the Burnside Expedition, Antietam, and his interactions with other Rhode Island soldiers. This book is exceptionally rare.

Cummings, S.S. *Life and Work of Rev. S.S. Cummings, Pastor, Chaplain, Delegate of Christian Commission, Missionary Agent of N.E. Home for Little Wanderers Twenty-Nine Years.* Sommerville, MA: NP, 1898.

Cummings served during the war as the chaplain of the Fourth Rhode Island. His letters home to his family is included in the book and provides interesting details regarding the service of a minister during the war.

Grandchamp, Robert. "Martyrs to the Cause of Liberty: Hopkinton Boys of the Fighting Fourth." *Rhode Island Roots* Vol. 40, No. 3 (September 2014), 135-143.

An interesting transcription and accompanying text of a long letter printed in the *Narragansett Weekly* of Westerly written by a soldier from Hopkinton who served in the Fourth. In the fall of 1861, nine students from the local Hopkinton Academy enlisted in the Fourth, four of whom would die in the Civil War. This article provides information on these men and their experiences at New Bern, Antietam, and in camp.

Nelson, Sebastian. "The Greene Brothers Civil War." *Military Images* Vol. 29, No. 3(November/December 2007), 28-33.

A very interesting photograph of the five Greene brothers who served in the Civil War. Daniel H. Greene served in the Fourth Rhode Island, while Willard served in the Twelfth Rhode Island Volunteers. Edward W. Greene was in the Twenty-Ninth Massachusetts, Jerome B. Greene in Battery I, First New York Artillery, and Henry A. Greene in the First California Infantry. Includes detailed analysis of the photograph and brief biographies of each brother.

Pullen, Drew. *Portrait of the Past: The Civil War on Roanoke Island North Carolina: A Pictorial Tour.* Mt. Holly, NJ: Aerial Perspective, 2002.

This is pictorial history of Roanoke Island, North Carolina, one of the early targets of the Burnside Expedition in February-March 1862. Filled with many modern photographs of the sites, as well as historical images and maps. Pullen quotes many letters in this volume from Captain William Chace of the Fourth Rhode Island who was later wounded at New Bern. The originals of the Chace letters are at the Rhode Island Historical Society.

Report of the Commissioner of the Fourth Regiment Rhode Island Volunteers to His Excellency Royal C. Taft, Governor of Rhode Island. Providence: E.L. Freeman & Son, 1889.

Further information regarding the Fourth Rhode Island clothing scandal.

Report of His Excellency George Peabody Wetmore, Governor, Relative to the Clothing Account of Fourth Regiment Rhode Island Volunteers, Etc. Providence: E.L. Freeman & Son, 1886.

When the Fourth Rhode Island was mustered in to the service in the fall of 1861, the men were charged $36.50 for their initial suit of military clothes; these should have been given free to the enlisted men. This is the first in a series of interesting pamphlets published by the state in which the veterans spent nearly thirty years trying to get their money back.

Shearman, Sumner U. *Battle of the Crater; and Experiences of Prison Life.* Providence: The Society, 1898.

Captain Shearman commanded a company in the Fourth Rhode Island and was captured at the Crater on July 30, 1864. In this important sketch, Shearman provides excellent detail into the role of the Fourth Rhode Island in the battle, as well as his subsequent imprisonment in Richmond. In one of the best quotes written by a

Rhode Island veteran, Shearman summed up his military service. "I have never regretted my being in the army during that most trying and critical period of our country. I feel as did the Westerner who said that he would not part with his experiences for a hundred thousand dollars, and he would not go through with it again for a hundred million."

Special Report of the Adjutant General in relation to the Reimbursement of the Members of the Late Fourth Rhode Island Volunteers, January 1st, 1892. Providence: E.L. Freeman & Son, 1892.

This pamphlet chronicles the resolution of the Fourth Rhode Island clothing scandal. In 1892, each veteran or their surviving family members was paid nearly one hundred dollars to settle the issue. This pamphlet provides a listing of surviving veterans of the Fourth.

Spooner, Henry Joshua. *The Maryland Campaign with the Fourth Rhode Island.* Providence: The Society, 1903.

A Brown University graduate, Spooner served as a lieutenant in the Fourth Rhode Island and later served five terms in the United States House of Representatives. The Maryland Campaign was the first for Spooner. He writes a superb narrative about being a new officer in a combat unit in the later summer of 1862. Spooner's work is a detailed and gripping account of the terrible ordeal endured by the Fourth Rhode Island in Otto's Cornfield at Antietam. Forming the extreme left flank of the Union Army, the Fourth sustained nearly fifty percent casualties when they were ambushed in the cornfield. This is one of the better publications of the Soldiers and Sailors Historical Society.

Thompson, Brian C. *Anthems and Minstrel Shows: The Life and Times of Calixa Lavall.e , 1842-1891.* Montreal: McGill-Queen's University Press, 2015.

Calixa Lavallee is perhaps the most famous man to serve in a Rhode Island regiment during the war. A Quebecois migrant, he performed in a well-received traveling show in the United States before the war. He enlisted in the band of the Fourth Rhode Island, served in the Burnside Expedition, and was wounded at Antietam; he was discharged shortly after. In 1880, Lavallee wrote the lyrics to "O, Canada," which later became the Canadian national anthem. This book is a full biography of Lavallee.

VanDenBossche, Kris. "War and Other Reminiscences." *Rhode Island History* Vol. 47, No. 4 (November 1989), 109-147.

One of the most detailed published memoirs written by a Rhode Island soldier, this is the transcribed and annotated memoirs of Hopkinton resident Sergeant George Bradford Carpenter of Company D of the Fourth Rhode Island; the original of these memoirs is housed at the Westerly Public Library. Carpenter wrote a detailed missive of his service with excellent details about the Burnside Expedition and the Battle of the Crater where he lost his arm.

Seventh Rhode Island Volunteers

Babbitt, Julia Emily. *Sketch of Major Jacob Babbitt, 7th Rhode Island Regiment.* Bristol, RI: NP, 1890.

A small biographical sketch written by Babbitt's daughter, this booklet provides important information on the beloved major of the Seventh Rhode Island who was mortally wounded at Fredericksburg. Babbitt was a prominent banker in Bristol before the war, had attended Norwich University, and had years of experience in the Rhode Island Militia. Also included is information on Babbitt Post # 15 of the Grand Army of the Republic in Bristol, named after the major.

Dietz, Claire Gilbert. "The Civil War Letters of Peleg G. Jones, Jr." *Rhode Island Roots* Vol. 34, No. 2 (June 2008), 76-90.

A corporal in Company I of the Seventh, Bristol native Peleg G. Jones wrote these interesting letters from his time in the Seventh. Especially detailed regarding the Seventh's service in the Western Theatre.

Grandchamp, Robert. "Balls and Shells fell in torants:" The Seventh Rhode Island Volunteers at the Battle of Fredericksburg." *Civil War Historian* Vol. 2, No. 5 (November/December 2006), 24-31.

Robert Grandchamp's earliest published article, based on a paper that he wrote at Rhode Island College for Dr. Stanley Lemons' Rhode Island History seminar. This article examines the Seventh's role at Fredericksburg and the devastating casualties they took there.

Grandchamp, Robert. "Company A, Seventh R.I. Volunteers at the Battle of Fredericksburg." *Rhode Island Roots* Vol. 40, No. 2 (June 2014), 97-106.

A very detailed letter written by Captain Lewis Leavens of Company A, chronicling the role his company played in the battle of Fredericksburg where the regiment sustained forty percent casualties including forty-nine soldiers killed or mortally wounded. The men in Company A were recruited from Charlestown, Hopkinton, Richmond, and Westerly. Also included is a list of men from the company who became casualties. Leavens wrote about the Seventh's terrible losses, "Scarce a man but had lost a friend or relative."

Grandchamp, Robert. "The First Deaths in the Seventh Rhode Island Volunteers in the Civil War." *Rhode Island Roots* Vol. 41, No. 2 (June 2015), 103-110.

Immediately after arriving in the South and being assigned to the Ninth Corps of the Army of the Potomac, a typhoid epidemic hit the ranks of the Seventh Rhode Island, killing several soldiers from Company A. This article chronicles the arrival of the Seventh in the South, the early deaths in the regiment, and how the Seventh responded by hosting an elaborate military funeral for the deceased soldiers from Hopkinton.

Grandchamp, Robert. "Joseph Weeden Burdick." *Rhode Island Roots* Vol. 40, No. 1 (March 2014), 41-44.

A detailed article about Private Joseph Weeden Burdick who served in Company A of the Seventh Rhode Island. Joining the Seventh with his two brothers-in-law, Burdick died of Yazoo Fever in Mississippi in July 1863.

Grandchamp, Robert. *From Providence to Fort Hell: Letters from Company K, Seventh Rhode Island Infantry.* Westminster, MD: Heritage Books, 2008.

One of the ten companies that composed the Seventh, Company K was recruited in the Pawtuxet Valley towns of Coventry, Scituate, and Foster. This book contains transcripts of letters written by six men who served in Company K. Each letter is transcribed as written by the soldier, while Grandchamp has added tremendously to the work by writing a narrative and identifying the people and places mentioned in each letter.

Grandchamp, Robert. "In Search of Private Coman." *Rhode Island Roots* Vol. 42, No. 4 (December 2016), 191-202.

Mortally wounded at Fredericksburg, Private William A. Coman of Company C, Seventh Rhode Island Volunteers was reported to his family as missing in action. His family never learned what truly happened to him. In this article, Grandchamp delves into the circumstances of Coman's wounding and why his final fate was never reported to his family.

Grandchamp, Robert. "Letters of Alfred Sheldon Knight of Scituate, Rhode Island." *Rhode Island Roots* Vol. 33, No. 3 (September 2007), 152-158.

A compilation of letters written by Private Knight who served in Company C of the Seventh. The son of a well-to-do dairy farmer,

Knight's letters provides interesting insight into the early service of the Seventh, as well as their participation at Fredericksburg. Alfred Sheldon Knight died of pneumonia at age twenty-nine on January 31, 1863.

Grandchamp, Robert. "The Letters of Major Peleg Edwin Peckham." *Rhode Island Roots,* Vol. 35, No. 1 (March 2009), 21-29.

Peckham served in Company A of the Seventh Rhode Island and rose to captain and brevet major; he was killed in action at Petersburg on April 2, 1865. His letters are quite remarkable in that shortly after the Union defeat at Fredericksburg and the issuing of the Emancipation Proclamation he thoroughly denounces President Abraham Lincoln and the cause of freeing the slaves. Over two years later however, after seeing extensive service in Mississippi and the Overland Campaign, Peckham recanted and wrote an impassioned letter to the *Providence Journal* urging Rhode Islanders to reelect President Lincoln as he believed him to be the only man who could properly restore the Union.

Grandchamp, Robert. "Lieutenant Colonel Job Arnold: An officer of rare judgment." *Rhode Island Roots* Vol. 43, No. 2 (June 2017), 101-108.

This biographical sketch studies the life and service of the Seventh's beloved lieutenant colonel, Job Arnold. Using family letters, Grandchamp recounts his service in the Union Army. Arnold contracted malaria in Mississippi in 1863 and died of the disease several years after the war ended.

Grandchamp, Robert. "My Lot to Fall:" The Final Letters of Major Jacob Babbitt." *Rhode Island Roots* Vol. 35, No. 2 (June 2009), 93-98.

A very interesting compilation of the last letters of Major Babbitt of the Seventh Rhode Island written shortly before and after the Battle of Fredericksburg; the originals are in the archives of

Fredericksburg-Spotsylvania National Military Park. Babbitt believed firmly in the Union cause and wrote to his wife, "Should it be my lot to fall, know that it was in defense of my beloved Constitution." These words would later serve as his epitaph.

Grandchamp, Robert. "My Lot to Fall: The Life and Death of Major Jacob Babbitt." *Military Images* Vol. 29, No. 3 (November/December 2007), 20-23.

A brief sketch of Major Babbitt, including several rare photographs of the major. One of Grandchamp's earliest works.

Grandchamp, Robert. *The Seventh Rhode Island Infantry in the Civil War.* Jefferson, NC: McFarland Publishing, 2007.

A heavily illustrated and deeply researched history of the Seventh Rhode Island, this book was Grandchamp's first successful publication. A well-written complement to Hopkins' original history, Grandchamp's book is a social history of the Seventh. Focusing on the soldiers from Hopkinton and Foster, he narrates their story through the conflict and the communities they left behind. Illustrated with many never before published photographs of Seventh Rhode Island veterans, Grandchamp uncovers the deep conflict often involving the regiment's officers, as well as highlighting the terrible casualties sustained by the Seventh at Fredericksburg and in Mississippi.

Grandchamp, Robert. *"We Lost Many Brave Men:" A Statistical History of the Seventh Rhode Island Volunteers.* Berwyn Heights, MD: Heritage Books, 2018.

A massive undertaking by Grandchamp, this book is a compiled roster of the men who served in the Seventh Rhode Island. Each soldier is listed, as is their fate. Filled with the detailed service of each man, Grandchamp has also identified the burial locations of nearly two thirds of the men who served in the Seventh Rhode Island.

Grandchamp, Robert. *With High and Holy Aim: Alfred Sheldon Knight and the Seventh Rhode Island Volunteers.* Frederick, MD: Publish America, 2006.

Robert Grandchamp's first published book, this is a biographical sketch of his great-great-great uncle who served in the Seventh Rhode Island. Researched from family papers, it includes transcripts of Knight's letters, as well as details regarding the early history of the Seventh. Also included is other information on Scituate Civil War soldiers.

Hopkins, William P. *The Seventh Regiment Rhode Island Volunteers in the Civil War, 1862-1865.* Providence: Snow & Farnum, 1903.

The most impressive of the post-war regimental histories published in Rhode Island, this book has often been cited as the most impressive regimental history ever published. Taking nearly a decade to research and write, the book follows the campaigns of the Seventh from its recruitment, to service with the Ninth Corps in Virginia and Mississippi, including the Battle of Fredericksburg where the regiment sustained forty percent casualties. Of particular use are the many biographies written about members of the regiment, filled with genealogical details and their service during the war. The book is heavily illustrated with hundreds of photographs of Seventh Rhode Island soldiers.

Lewis, Nathan B., William P. Hopkins, and Elisha C. Knight. *Report of the Rhode Island- Vicksburg Monument Commission to the General Assembly 1909.* Providence: Snow & Farnum, 1909.

A detailed report to the Rhode Island General Assembly regarding the bidding, construction, and the dedication of the Seventh Rhode Island Monument at Vicksburg National Battlefield. The memorial was dedicated on November 11, 1908 with several veterans and dignitaries from Rhode Island in attendance.

Nowotarski, Steve. "The Diary of Tryphena Clarke Cundall."
    Rhode Island Roots Vol. 25, No. 4 (December 1999),
    153-172.

One of the more interesting Civil War diaries kept by a Rhode Islander. Cundall was a widow who lived in the Ashaway section of Hopkinton. She was also the mother of two soldiers; one of her sons served three months in the Ninth Rhode Island, while another, Isaac served three years in the Seventh Rhode Island and survived. Her diary covers the period 1862-1889, but the bulk of the journal covers the Civil War years. Tryphena poured her heart into her writings and they are quite emotional as she writes of Isaac's experiences in the Seventh Rhode Island.

Peckham, Stephen Farnum. "*Recollections of a Hospital Steward
    During the Civil War.*" *Journal of American History* Vol.
    18 (1924), 151-158, 275-282, 335-341.

Originally read as a paper before the Rhode Island Soldiers and Sailors Historical Society, this paper was posthumously published in the *Journal of American History*. In this important memoir, Peckham provides details regarding the medical staff of the Seventh Rhode Island and the problems faced by the doctors of the regiment treating patients suffering battle wounds and from disease. During the war Peckham was also a correspondent to the *Providence Journal*. Peckham wrote candidly about the officers of the regiment and provides excellent details regarding the feud between Lieutenant Colonel Percy Daniels and Major Ethan Amos Jenks. The original manuscript of these recollections is at the Newport Historical Society.

*Report of Rhode Island Commissioners of the Vicksburg National
    Military Park Commission, to His Excellency Charles
    Dean Kimball, Governor, at the January Session, 1902.*
    Providence: E.L. Freeman & Sons, 1903.

In 1900, the Rhode Island General Assembly authorized funding to erect a monument to be erected to honor the Seventh Rhode Island. In 1901, Major Ethan Amos Jenks and Drummer William

P. Hopkins traveled to Vicksburg and visited old sites connected with the regiment's service there, while looking for a suitable site to erect the monument. This is the report of their trip. The monument was dedicated in Vicksburg in 1908.

Smith, Thomas T., Jerry D. Thompson, Robert Wooster, and Ben E. Pingenot. *The Reminiscences of Major General Zenas R. Bliss, 1854-1876: From the Texas Frontier to the Civil War and Back Again.* Austin: Texas State Historical Association, 2007.

A native of Johnston and a graduate of West Point, Zenas Randall Bliss served as the colonel of the Tenth and Seventh Rhode Island Regiments. He was awarded the Medal of Honor for his heroism at Fredericksburg. Bliss' memoirs provide details regarding his service on the Texas frontier both before and after the Civil War. The Civil War sections are particularly detailed and provide a very important first-person account of the Seventh Rhode Island's role at Fredericksburg and in the Mississippi Campaign.

White, Gerald T. *Baptism in Oil: Stephen F. Peckham in Southern California 1865-66.* San Francisco: Book Club of San Francisco, 1984.

Peckham served in the war as the hospital steward of the Seventh Rhode Island. After the war, he traveled the country prospecting in oil and became one of the nation's earliest experts in the petroleum industry. This book provides a very good example of the postwar activities of a Rhode Island Civil War veteran.

Ninth Rhode Island Volunteers

Spicer, William A. *History of the Ninth and Tenth Regiments Rhode Island Volunteers, and the Tenth Rhode Island Battery, in the Union Army in 1862.* Providence: Snow & Farnum, 1892.

An anecdotal history of the Ninth and Tenth Regiments during their three months of service in the defenses of Washington in the summer of 1862. Hastily raised and sent to the front, these two regiments accomplished little during their term of service. Spicer's history is a good history of life in camp, the trials of soldier life, and the interesting people the soldiers encountered. The book is well illustrated, largely with engravings copied from the book *Si Klegg and His Pard*. Also includes the activities of the veteran's associations of the Ninth and Tenth.

Tenth Rhode Island Volunteers

Fitzpatrick, Mike. "John Bradford of the U.S. Signal Corps."
    Military Images Vol. 23, No. 3 (November/December 2001), 17.

A rare photograph and brief article about Bradford who served in the First, Tenth, and Eleventh Rhode Island Regiments, and then enlisted in the United States Signal Corps.

"From the Collections." *Rhode Island History* Vol. 39, No. 4
    (November 1980), 131-132.

The Burnside Zouaves were part of the Rhode Island Militia that wore the distinctive North African inspired Zouave dress. A well-drilled unit, the Burnside Zouaves put on drill demonstrations in Providence throughout the war and saw active service as Company H of the Tenth Rhode Island, minus their distinctive uniforms. This article includes three detailed photographs of the Burnside Zouaves.

Spicer, William A. *The High School Boys of the Tenth R.I.*
    Regiment with a Roll of Teachers and Students of the Providence High School who served in the Army or Navy of the United States during the Rebellion.
    Providence: N. Bang Williams, 1883.

Company B of the Tenth Rhode Island was commanded by former Rhode Island Governor Elisha Dyer Sr. It was composed mostly of students from Brown University and teenagers from Providence High School. This sketch chronicles the camp life of the company in Washington in the summer of 1862. Among their actions was the capture of a small howitzer, named the "Tenallytown Gun," that is still in the possession of the Rhode Island National Guard. Also included is a list of the students of the school that served in the military during the Civil War. An informative study.

Spicer, William A. *History of the Ninth and Tenth Regiments Rhode Island Volunteers, and the Tenth Rhode Island Battery, in the Union Army in 1862.* Providence: Snow & Farnum, 1892.

Spicer, a high school student from Providence served in Company B. See above entry under the Ninth Rhode Island Volunteers for full description.

Eleventh Rhode Island Volunteers

Archambault, Alan H. "11th Rhode Island Volunteer Infantry, 1862-1863." *Military Collector & Historian* Vol. 53, No. 4 (Winter 2001-2002), 184-185.

A noted military artist, this brief article by Archambault is a compilation of the various uniforms worn by the Eleventh Rhode Island during their nine-month service.

Mowry, William A. *Camp Life in the Civil War, Eleventh R.I. Infantry.* Boston: NP, 1914.

Mowry served as the principal of Providence High School before and after his service; he was the captain of Company K of the Eleventh. Written and published shortly before his death, this small book provides a fascinating look at soldier life. Mowry remembered small details of his service and this book is a fantastic glimpse into the life of a Union soldier on campaign.

Nickerson, Ansel D. *A Raw Recruit's War Experiences.* Providence: Printed by the Press Company, 1888.

During his nine-month service, Nickerson was a frequent correspondent to the *Pawtucket Times*. Heavily involved in the Grand Army of the Republic after the war, this book was based on a lecture he originally delivered before the Soldiers and Sailors Historical Society; this book however was independently published by Nickerson and not the Society. Very popular in its day, this book provides a good view of soldiering in the Eleventh Rhode Island, especially their service around Suffolk, Virginia in the spring of 1863.

Parkhurst, Charles H. *Incidents of Service with the Eleventh Regiment Rhode Island Volunteers.* Providence: Sidney S. Rider, 1883.

Parkhurst served as a captain in the Eleventh Rhode Island. This sketch recalls the conditions in the country that led Lincoln to call for the nine-month regiments in the fall of 1862, as well as the massive response by Rhode Island to fill the Eleventh and Twelfth regiments. Parkhurst also discusses life in camp, and the regiment's actions at Suffolk in 1863 shortly before they were mustered out.

Remington, George H. *A Statistical History of Co. I, 11th R.I. Volunteers: Together with an account of its 20th Reunion, holden on the grounds of the Warwick Club, Friday, July 13, 1883.* Providence: E.A. Johnson & Co., 1884.

A small booklet that chronicles the men of Company I of the Eleventh Rhode Island. It provides a roster, and lists the fate of each man since the war ended, as well as company reunion activities. Also included are several pages of poetry by two members of the company.

Thompson, J.C. *History of the Eleventh Regiment, Rhode Island Volunteers, in the War of the Rebellion.* Providence: Committee of the Eleventh Regiment Veteran Association, 1881.

Published under the pseudonym "R.W. Rock," this book is perhaps the poorest regimental history published by a Rhode Island infantry regiment. The book covers the recruiting and service of the regiment but does not provide significant details of the regiment's actions.

Twelfth Rhode Island Volunteers

Diman, George Waters. *Autobiography and Travels by Sea and Land.* Bristol: Bristol Phenix, 1896.

A sailor before the war, Diman served in Company E of the Twelfth, raised in Bristol County. His memoirs provide a good understanding of the Twelfth's service and their role at Fredericksburg. Although he only served nine months, Diman's health never recovered from his brief time in the army.

Grandchamp, Robert. "Letters of Frank J. Wilder." *Rhode Island Roots* Vol. 33, No. 2 (June 2007), 93-100.

Grandchamp, Robert. "Letters of Frank J. Wilder Part II. *Rhode Island Roots* Vol. 33, No. 4 (December 2007), 209-211.

Two articles containing transcriptions and information on Private Frank J. Wilder. A member of Company A of the Twelfth Rhode Island, Wilder was abandoned by his parents at an early age and raised by an aunt in Scituate. His letters contain good details on soldier life and the Battle of Fredericksburg. Wilder died of typhoid in January 1863 and is buried in Scituate.

Grant, Joseph W. *The Flying Regiment: Journal of the Campaign of the 12th Regt. Rhode Island Volunteers*. Providence: S.S. Rider & Bro., 1865.

A native of Cumberland, Grant served in Company F of the Twelfth. This book provides a detailed narrative of the nine-month service of the regiment and was published immediately after the war ended. Of particular interest is Grant's detailed account of fighting guerilas in Kentucky in the spring and early summer of 1863.

Lapham, Oscar. *Recollections of Service in the Twelfth Regiment, R.I. Volunteers*. Providence: The Society, 1885.

Written by a captain in the Twelfth, this interesting account narrates the recruiting and service of the Twelfth. Captain Lapham provides a good account of Fredericksburg, as well as subsequent service in Kentucky chasing Confederate guerillas. As with the Tillinghast narrative below, this account was later published in the regimental history of the Twelfth Rhode Island. Lapham later served two terms in the United States House of Representatives.

Tillinghast, Pardon E. *History of the Twelfth Regiment Rhode Island Volunteers in the Civil War 1862-1863*. Providence: Snow & Farnum, 1904.

The history of the Twelfth Rhode Island was written by a committee of members of the regiment and edited by Tillinghast. Rather than being a flowing narrative, the book is the memoirs of several different soldiers arranged by chapter. The format, while different from other regimental histories allows more than one voice to tell the story of the regiment. The history of the Twelfth is well illustrated and tells the story of the regiment at Fredericksburg and during their term of service in the West. While most Rhode Island soldiers wrote home that the Twelfth broke and ran under fire at Fredericksburg, this book presents a heroic version on their actions at the battle.

Tillinghast, Pardon E. *Reminiscences of Service with the Twelfth Rhode Island Volunteers, and a Memorial of Col. George H. Browne.* Providence: The Society, 1885.

Tillinghast served as the quartermaster sergeant of the Twelfth. Much of the material in this narrative was later reprinted in his regimental history of the regiment. Also included in this publication is a biographical sketch of Colonel George H. Browne. A congressman from Glocester, with no prior military experience, Browne was one of the poorer regimental commanders sent from Rhode Island, but was extremely popular with his men.

Chapter Five:

Light Artillery Sources

First Rhode Island Light Artillery Regiment

Bucklyn, John K. *Battle of Cedar Creek, October 19, 1864.*
    Providence: Sidney S. Rider, 1883.

Bucklyn was a lieutenant in Battery E, but was assigned to the Sixth Corps Artillery Brigade on staff duty. The brigade was commanded by the colonel of the First Rhode Island Light Artillery Regiment, Charles H. Tompkins of Providence; he was severely wounded at Cedar Creek. During the engagement, Batteries C and G of Rhode Island were assigned to help hold back the Confederate line; they did so, but at a very high cost. This narrative provides a detailed view of the battle, as seen by a staff officer, while relating the role of the two Rhode Island batteries in the engagement.

Ferguson, Cynthia Comery and Jane Lancaster. "The Providence
    Marine Corps of Artillery in the Civil War." *Rhode Island
    History* Vol. 60, No. 2 (Spring 2002), 55-66.

The Providence Marine Corps of Artillery was given the title "Mother of Batteries" as the organization was responsible for the raising and training of all ten batteries sent to the front by Rhode Island during the Civil War. This article chronicles the raising of those batteries, as well as illustrating prominent Rhode Islanders who served in the Providence Marine Corps of Artillery.

Grandchamp, Robert, Cynthia Ferguson, and Jane Lancaster.
    *"Rhody Redlegs:" A History of the Providence Marine
    Corps of Artillery and the 103d Field Artillery, Rhode
    Island Army National Guard, 1901-2010.* Jefferson, NC:
    McFarland Publishing, 2011.

Originally begun as a bicentennial history in 2001 by Ferguson and Lancaster, Grandchamp completed the project from 2008-2010. This is a full history of the Providence Marine Corps Artillery and its successor unit, the 103rd Field Artillery of the Rhode Island National Guard. Heavily illustrated, pertinent chapters contend with the Dorr Rebellion, how the corps prepared for the Civil War, and its operations in the Civil War as the First Rhode Island Light Artillery. Additional chapters cover World War I, World War II, Korea, and the War on Terror. A complete history of this illustrious unit.

Hartwell, Everett S. *An Historical Sketch of the Providence Marine Corps of Artillery 1801-1951: Given at the celebration of the 150th Anniversary of the Corps at the Benefit Street Armory, Providence, R.I. February 12, 1952*. Providence: Providence Journal, 1952.

A detailed, albeit brief sketch of the Providence Marine Corps of Artillery for their sesquicentennial in 1952. Provides good information on the early days of the corps.

Monroe, John Albert. *Reminiscences of the War of the Rebellion of 1861-5*. Providence: N. Bang Williams, 1881.

This publication is Monroe's overall memoirs of the war and does not provide as much detail as some of his writings on Battery D. After Antietam, Monroe became a field officer and commanded an artillery training camp, as well as an artillery brigade later in the war. Provides a useful source of information on artillery tactics and Monroe's ability to command larger units.

Peck, George B. *Historical Address Delivered at the Dedication of the Memorial Tablet on the Arsenal Benefit Street, Corner of Meeting Providence, R.I. Thursday July 19, 1917*. Providence: Rhode Island Print Co., 1917.

In 1917, as the United States prepared to enter World War I, the veterans of the First Rhode Island Light Artillery Regiment dedicated a memorial tablet to their comrades who served in the regiment; it still is present on the arsenal, and has since been joined by plaques commemorating service in World War I, World War II, Korea, and Iraq. This small publication provides a thumbnail sketch of each battery, as well as chronicling the lineage of the Providence Marine Corps of Artillery and the current 103rd Field Artillery Regiment.

Battery A

Aldrich, Thomas M. *The History of Battery A, First Regiment Rhode Island Light Artillery in the War to Preserve the Union, 1861-1865.* Providence: Snow & Farnum, 1904.

The last published battery history and the only one to be illustrated with photographs rather than engravings. Aldrich's history of Battery A is well regarded, however one must compare Aldrich against other sources, such as *Diary of Battery A*. Aldrich often placed himself at the center of the action, such as at Bull Run and Gettysburg when he was actually in the rear with the supply train. This book provides a very good view of Battery A's actions at Antietam.

Child, Benjamin H. *From Fredericksburg to Gettysburg.* Providence: The Society, 1895.

Child received the Medal of Honor for heroism at Antietam and later became chief of police in Providence. This narrative covers Battery A's participation in the Gettysburg Campaign of June-July 1863. Assigned to the Artillery Brigade of the Second Corps, Battery A had a long, tedious march to Pennsylvania. They were heavily engaged on July 3, 1863 during Pickett's Charge. This account provides an excellent understanding of Battery A's action at the Angle during the assault.

Grandchamp, Robert. "Thomas Aldrich, Company A, and the Controversy at the Angle." *Gettysburg Magazine* 39 (July 2008), 71-82.

Analyzing a series of letters written after the war by the veterans of Battery B, Grandchamp analyzes the writings of Thomas Aldrich, including his history of Battery A to conclude that Aldrich lied about much of his Civil War service. A heavily researched article about Battery A at Gettysburg.

Kowalis, Jeff. "Brave Walk a Heap: The Tragic Life of William Henry Walcott, Sergeant, Battery A, 1st Rhode Island Artillery, Captain, 17th U.S. Infantry." *Military Images* Vol. 18, No. 4 (November/December 1998), 36-39.

A brief biography and accompanying photograph of Captain William H. Walcott. A native of Providence, Walcott originally served in Battery A before joining the Seventeenth United States Infantry. He lost a leg fighting in the Valley of Death at Gettysburg and later saw service on the western frontier. He died in 1901 and is buried at Arlington.

Monroe, John Albert. *The Rhode Island Artillery at the First Battle of Bull Run.* Providence: Sidney S. Rider, 1878.

A lively narrative of Battery A's mustering and participation at Bull Run. This was Monroe's first engagement and he writes a gripping narrative of the artillery fight between Battery A on Matthew's Hill and John Imboden's Virginia Battery. Also covered is the controversy regarding who saved the Bull Run Gun from capture. That gun, a James Rifle is now at the Rhode Island State House.

Reichardt, Theodore. *Diary of Battery A, First Regiment Rhode Island Light Artillery.* Providence: N.B. Williams, 1865.

Published shortly after returning home from the war, this book is the remarkable field diary of Reichardt who served in Battery A. Written on the field, and unedited by time and memory, these diary entries provide a crucial view of the Rhode Island artillery in camp and on the battlefield. This book is the best source of information for Battery A.

Trinque, Bruce A. "Arnold's Battery and the 26th North
    Carolina." *Gettysburg Magazine* 12 (January 1995), 61-
    67.

In his regimental history of Battery A, author Thomas Aldrich wrote that his unit fired one last salvo of canister into the ranks of the 26th North Carolina during the climactic struggle at the Angle during Pickett's Charge. The Carolinians, after receiving the blast retreated in disarray. To commemorate the event, the State of North Carolina placed a monument in front of Battery A's position on Cemetery Ridge. In this very detailed article, Trinque analyzes available sources and concludes that Aldrich was wrong about what happened and that Battery A actually faced a Tennessee regiment. Despite his research, the North Carolina monument still stands.

Turgeon, Sandra A. *All Quiet on the Rappahannock Tonight: The*
    Civil War Letters of Lt. Peter Hunt 1861-1864, 1st Rhode
    Island Light Artillery. East Providence: East
    Providence Historical Society, 2017.

Lieutenant Hunt was originally a member of Battery C, before becoming a lieutenant in Battery A shortly after Antietam. His letters have been in the collection of the East Providence Historical Society for many years and this book is a compilation of his letters. Hunt wrote honestly and deeply regarding his service in the Army of the Potomac. These letters provide an in-depth look into the First Rhode Island Light Artillery, as well as the engagements he participated in. Unfortunately, the editing is not particularly strong; there is little narration and the people and places are not identified and annotated in the volume. Despite this, these letters are an important contribution to the field. Hunt was mortally wounded at Cold Harbor.

Battery B

Grandchamp, Robert. "The appearance of a gang of Chinamen: A
    Study of the Uniforms worn by Brown's Battery B, First

Rhode Island Light Artillery." *Military Collector and Historian* Vol. 59, No. 1 (Spring 2007), 58-64.

An analysis of the many different styles of uniforms worn by Battery B during service with the Army of the Potomac. Includes many images of Battery B members.

Grandchamp, Robert. "Brown's Battery B, First Rhode Island Light Artillery at the Battle of Gettysburg." *Gettysburg Magazine* 36 (January 2007), 86-94.

Battery B was heavily engaged during July 2 and July 3, 1863 at Gettysburg. This article provides an in-depth analysis of Battery B's actions on both days of the battle, as well as how the veterans of Battery B remembered their service at Gettysburg.

Rhodes, John H. *The Gettysburg Gun.* Providence: The Society, 1892.

During the Battle of Gettysburg, a light twelve pounder Napoleon cannon of Battery B was struck at the muzzle by a Confederate shell, killing two members of the gun crew. When Sergeant Albert Straight tried to load the cannon, a cannon ball became stuck in the muzzle and the gun was sent to the rear. Today it is known as the Gettysburg Gun and is on display at the Rhode Island State House. This narrative, written by Rhodes who was present at Gettysburg, and witnessed the event recalls Straight's actions at Gettysburg. Also included is information about the veteran's efforts to have the gun returned to Rhode Island, and the 1874 ceremony to mark its return.

Rhodes, John H. *The History of Battery B, First Regiment Rhode Island Light Artillery, in the War to Preserve the Union, 1861-1865.* Providence: Snow & Farnham, 1894.

One of the better battery histories from Rhode Island, Rhodes provides a detailed narrative of Battery B's service in the Army of the Potomac. The book includes much minutiae relating to the life of a Union artilleryman. Illustrated with engravings, this book provides much relevant information on Battery B's actions at Gettysburg and the Gettysburg Gun, now on display at the Rhode Island State House.

Straight, Charles Tillinghast. *Battery B, First R.I. Light Artillery, August 13-1861-June 12, 1865.* Central Falls: E.L. Freeman, 1907.

Charles Tillinghast Straight was the son of Sergeant Albert Straight who placed the cannonball in the Gettysburg Gun now at the Rhode Island State House. Although his father died in the Civil War, Straight devoted his life to researching and corresponding with the soldiers of Rhode Island; unfortunately, only a handful of his papers now appear in private hands. This is an interesting booklet that Straight compiled about Battery B. In it he presents a brief history of the unit, but more importantly provides excellent information regarding the fates of those who died in the war, as well as the postwar homes of many of the men. Straight served as secretary of the Battery B Veterans Association for many years.

Battery C

Grandchamp, Robert. "The Case of James A. Matteson of Scituate, R.I." *Rhode Island Roots* Vol. 42, No. 3 (September 2016), 159-168.

A very detailed study of the life, service, and death of a soldier in Battery C. Matteson was killed in action at Cedar Creek in October of 1864 but was confused by authorities with another soldier of the same name from Battery G. Using pension records, Grandchamp is able to untangle the mystery and reveal what actually happened to this soldier.

Stone, Edwin W. *Rhode Island in the Rebellion.* Providence: G.H. Whitney, 1864.

A war correspondent for the *Providence Journal,* Stone's letters from Battery C is the most detailed source of information regarding the unit. The letters are highly readable and enlightening. In addition, the appendix contains regimental histories of each Rhode Island unit. Later reprinted in 1865 with an addendum covering the 1864 campaigns.

Battery D

Monroe, John Albert. *Battery D, First Rhode Island Light Artillery at the Battle of Antietam, September 17, 1862.* Providence: The Society, 1886.

An Antietam, Battery D was one of the first Union units engaged in the savage early morning fighting at Miller's Cornfield and Dunker Church. This narrative by Monroe is easily his best, and one of the finest accounts of the early fighting at Antietam. The account is very detailed, and Monroe writes about the many men Battery D lost during the engagement. Monroe stated that because Battery D was recruited largely from the rural parts of the state, it's actions at Antietam were never fully appreciated. Of note, the captain wrote that the officers of Battery D were eating jonny cakes prior to the battle, a well-known dish among Rhode Islanders!

Monroe, John Albert. *Battery D, First Rhode Island Light Artillery at the Second Battle of Bull Run.* Providence: The Society, 1890.

Assigned to the First Corps of the Army of the Potomac for the 1862 campaigns, Battery D saw heavy action at Second Manassas from August 28-30, 1862 in its baptism by fire. This detailed account by battery commander, Captain Monroe provides an excellent account of Battery D in the battle.

Sumner, George C. *Battery D, First Rhode Island Light Artillery, in the Civil War, 1861- 1865.* Providence: Rhode Island Printing Company, 1897.

One of the smaller battery histories. Sumner died in the middle of writing this book and it was finished by an unknown colleague. This factor, combined with the loss of Battery D's official papers which were captured at Cedar Creek make this one of the poorer battery histories. Of value however is the detailed roster. For specifics on Battery D's campaigns, readers should consult the several publications from Battery D veterans published by the Soldiers and Sailors Historical Society.

Sumner, George C., George B. Peck, and Edward P. Tobie. *John Albert Monroe: A Memorial.* Providence: The Society, 1892.

After mustering out of the service in the fall of 1864, Monroe returned to Providence and became a prominent civil engineer. He remained active in the Providence Marine Corps of Artillery, as well as the Grand Army of the Republic, and the Soldiers and Sailors Historical Society. This sketch of his life was written by Sumner who served under him in Battery D. Peck and Tobie spoke at Monroe's funeral, and the eulogy and services are also included in this interesting volume of a beloved Rhode Island soldier.

Sumner, George C. *Recollections of Service in Battery D, First Rhode Island Light Artillery.* Providence: The Society, 1891.

Sumner's memoirs of service in Battery D. Much of this material was later reincorporated into his regimental history.

Parker, Ezra K. *Campaign of Battery D, First Rhode Island Light Artillery, in Kentucky and East Tennessee.* Providence: The Society, 1913.

Following their transfer to Kentucky in the spring of 1863, Battery D, and the bulk of the Ninth Corps were sent to Knoxville, Tennessee in the fall of 1863 to protect Union loyalists in the area. The battery went on to play an important role at the Battle of Campbell's Station and in the defense of Knoxville in November 1863. Parker provides a very detailed sketch of Battery D in the campaign, as well as the privations suffered by the men while encamped near Knoxville.

Tanner, David B. *"Our Limbs are Lost! Our Country Saved!" A Short Sketch of the Service and Sacrifices of David B. Tanner, Late of the 5th Rhode Island Battery, Who Lost His Leg at the Battle of Antietam, Sept. 17th 1862.* Boston: John D. Flagg & Co., 1870.

Published as a means to raise funds to support his family and sold for twenty-five cents, Tanner's sketch provides some good information regarding Battery D's service at Antietam, where Tanner lost his leg.

Battery E

Butts, Francis B. *The Organization and First Campaign of Battery E, First Rhode Island Light Artillery.* Providence: The Society, 1896.

Battery E was recruited largely in western Rhode Island, and had a different make up than the other batteries of the regiment. In this account, Butts narrates the recruiting and drilling of Battery E in Rhode Island before their assignment to the Third Corps early in the war. In addition, he writes a detailed account of Battery E's participation in the Peninsula Campaign and the Seven Days Battles.

Lewis, George. *The History of Battery E, First Regiment Rhode Island Light Artillery, in the War of 1861 and 1865, to Preserve the Union.* Providence: Snow & Farnham, 1892.

Perhaps the best of the six published battery histories from Rhode Island, Lewis' history of Battery E is a model history. Heavily illustrated with engravings, the book includes the detailed memoirs of several members, as well as excellent biographical details of battery members. Lewis does an excellent job of placing Battery E's actions within the context of the Army of the Potomac's campaigns.

Parker, Ezra K. *From the Rapidan to the James under Grant.* Providence: The Society, 1909.

During the Overland Campaign, Battery E was part of the Sixth Corps Artillery Brigade. This interesting account, one of the few published by the Soldiers and Sailors Historical Society about the Overland Campaign recalls the harrowing forty days of non-stop combat as Lee battled Grant. Of particular note are Parker's comments regarding the role of artillery in the campaign.

Usler, Steve. "Cavern of Horrors." *Civil War Historian* Vol. 4, No. 2 (March/April 2008), 18-23.

In this article, Usler, a retired army non-commissioned officer, traces the post-Gettysburg experiences of Lieutenant John Knight Bucklyn of Battery E. Severely wounded on July 2, 1863, Bucklyn wrote his post-war memoirs as a series of articles in the North Kingstown *Standard Times*. Usler uses these memoirs to build his narrative. Bucklyn survived his wounds and later became a school principal in Connecticut; in 1899, he was belatedly awarded the Medal of Honor for heroism at Chancellorsville.

Battery F

Chase, Philip S. *Battery F, First Regiment Rhode Island Light Artillery in the Civil War, 1861-1865*. Providence: Snow & Farnham, 1892.

The only battery to not spend any of its service in the Army of the Potomac, Battery F spent the majority of the war in North Carolina and joined the Army of the James in Virginia in 1864. This book provides an interesting look into combat in the North Carolina theatre, as well as the participation of Battery F in several smaller engagements along the coast. Illustrated with engravings and includes a useful roster.

Chase, Philip S. *Organization and Service of Battery F, First Rhode Island Light Artillery, to January 1st 1863*. Providence: N. Bang Williams, 1880.

Covering the early history of Battery F, much of this material was later incorporated by Chase into his regimental history of the unit.

Chase, Philip S. *Service with Battery F, First Rhode Island Light Artillery in North Carolina.* Providence: The Society, 1884.

This sketch covers the history of Battery F for most of 1863 and 1864, before their transfer to the Army of the James in April 1864. Chase provides a good overview of garrison life in North Carolina following the Burnside Expedition and the Goldsboro Raid of December 1862. As with the above sketch, much of this material was later incorporated into the regimental history.

Simpson, Thomas. *My Four Months' Experience as a Prisoner of War.* Providence: The Society, 1883.

Written by the captain of Battery F, this narrative relates his capture near Petersburg and his imprisonment in Richmond in the fall of 1864.

Battery G

Grandchamp, Robert. "The Artillery at Granite Hill." *The Artilleryman* Vol. 30, No. 2 (Spring 2009), 5-9.

A detailed tactical study about the July 5, 1863 near Granite Hill, west of Gettysburg during the Confederate retreat. During the engagement, the Sixth Corps Artillery Brigade, including Battery G contributed greatly to driving the Confederate Second Corps back towards the Potomac.

Grandchamp, Robert. "Battery G, 1st Rhode Island, Earned 17 Medals at Petersburg, April 2, '65." *The Artilleryman* Vol. 29, No. 4 (Fall 2008), 19-25.

A detailed study of Battery G's actions on April 2, 1865 at the storming of Petersburg that led to seven members of the battery being awarded the Medal of Honor. Also includes details about how the Medal of Honor was awarded to the veterans in the decades after the Civil War.

Grandchamp, Robert. *The Boys of Adams' Battery G: The Civil War through the eyes of a Union light artillery unit.* J Jefferson, NC: McFarland Publishing, 2009.

In this masterful study, Robert Grandchamp writes a full regimental history of Battery G; one of the few units never to publish a history. Based on intense, in-depth research, Grandchamp chronicles the organization, campaigns, and personalities of the battery and the many battles they took part in. Well illustrated with many images of battery members, this book follows Battery G's path as they took part in every major battle with the Army of the Potomac. One of the finest books ever written about Rhode Island and the Civil War.

Grandchamp, Robert. "The Civil War Letters of George Lee Gaskell." M.A. Thesis, Rhode Island College, 2010.

This deeply researched thesis is composed of the transcribed and annotated letters of George Lee Gaskell. A native of Sterling, Connecticut, Gaskell served in Battery G and later became a lieutenant in the Fourteenth Rhode Island Heavy Artillery. These letters are riveting and filled with many details regarding Gaskell's service, the battles he was in, and the flora and fauna he encountered. Also included is a detailed essay about Civil War soldier's letters. This thesis was later published as *A Connecticut Yankee at War*.

Battery H

Fenner, Earl. *The History of Battery H, First Regiment Rhode Island Light Artillery, in the War to Preserve the Union, 1861-1865.* Providence: Snow & Farnham, 1894.

Battery H spent much of the war in garrison duty around Washington and only went to the front lines at Petersburg late in the war. This regimental history is most useful for understanding how the First Rhode Island Light Artillery was recruited. This book is also illustrated with engravings and enlightened with detailed biographical sketches.

First Rhode Island Battery

No separately published history, refer to Woodbury, *A Narrative of the Campaign of the First Rhode Island Regiment* for roster of battery members and their service in the Shenandoah Valley in June-July 1861.

Tenth Rhode Island Battery

No separately published regimental history, refer to Spicer, *History of the Ninth and Tenth Rhode Island Volunteers, and the Tenth Rhode Island Battery, in the Union Army in 1862* for a battery roster and brief chapter regarding their three-month service.

Chapter Six:

Heavy Artillery Sources

Third Rhode Island Heavy Artillery

Carlson, Kenneth S. "White and Black: The Third and Fourteenth Heavy Artilleries: A socioeconomic and military profile." B.A. Thesis, Rhode Island College, 1995.

A thoroughly researched and well-written bachelor's thesis, this is a comparative study of Rhode Island's white and black heavy artillery units during the Civil War. Carlson conducted in-depth research and provides excellent statistical information regarding the soldiers of both regiments, as well as their combat operations. After graduating from Rhode Island College, Carlson took a position as a reference archivist at the Rhode Island State Archives in Providence and spent much of his career organizing, cataloging, and researching the official papers relating to Rhode Island and the Civil War from the governor's office, as well as the adjutant general.

Denison, Frederic. *A Chaplain's Experiences in the Union Army.* Providence: The Society, 1893.

In this biographical sketch, Denison relates the role of the chaplain in the Union Army, as well as his experiences serving as the regimental chaplain in the First Rhode Island Cavalry and the Third Rhode Island Heavy Artillery.

Denison, Frederic. *Shot and Shell: The Third Rhode Island Heavy Artillery Regiment in the Rebellion, 1861-1865: Camps, Forts, Batteries, Garrisons, Marches, Skirmishes, Sieges, Battles, and Victories, Also, the Roll of Honor and Roll of the Regiment: Illustrated with Portrait, Maps, and Scenes*. Providence: J.A. & R.A. Reid, 1879.

One of the best books written about a heavy artillery regiment, Denison's volume is a fantastic regimental history. He covers provides information on each of the twelve batteries of the regiment and their varied service from Florida to Virginia. Highly readable, *Shot and Shell* also includes information on the effectiveness of heavy artillery during the war, as well as the recruiting of the regiment.

Egan, Patrick. *The Florida Campaign with Light Battery C, Third Rhode Island Heavy Artillery*. Providence: The Society, 1905.

Although the Third Rhode Island was designated as a heavy artillery regiment, Batteries A and C of the regiment served in the field as light artillery. Light Battery C was heavily engaged at Olustee, Florida on February 20, 1864. This sketch narrates the role of Battery C in the engagement and how they managed to save all their guns from capture.

Hammerstrom, Kirsten. "Souvenirs of War." *Rhode Island History* Vol.70, No. 2 (Summer/Fall 2012), 75-86.

Sergeant George M. Turner served in Battery A of the Third Rhode Island Heavy Artillery. In 1930, a family member left his wartime relics to the Rhode Island Historical Society. This article provides illustrates of some of those items, as well as quoting from several of Turner's letters which are in the collection of the Providence Public Library.

James, Martin S. *War Reminiscences*. Providence: The Society, 1911.

The very detailed memoirs of Captain James who commanded Light Battery C of the Third Rhode Island Heavy Artillery. James originally helped raise a company in Cumberland for the Second Rhode Island, but illness prevented him taking the field; instead he was commissioned into the Third Rhode Island. A superb overview of early war recruiting in Rhode Island, as well as James' experiences commanding Light Battery C at Petersburg late in the war.

Irwin, David. *Brief Biographical Sketch: Also Narrative of Service in the Civil War, with the 10th Army Corps, Department of the South, and Army of the James.* San Francisco: NP, 1908.

A small booklet published by First Lieutenant David Irwin who served in Battery F of the Third Rhode Island Heavy Artillery. Provides some interesting information regarding his early life in Providence, as well as his service in the Third serving during the siege of Fort Pulaski, as well as service against Fort Wagner and Fort Sumter. After the war, Lieutenant Irwin moved to San Francisco.

Lee, Thomas Zanlaur. "Chief Egan's War Record Written for State Archives." *The Journal of the American Irish Historical Society* Volume 8 (1909), 177-182.

Patrick Egan was only fifteen when he enlisted in the Third Rhode Island Heavy Artillery in August 1861. He survived the war unscathed and was mustered out as a sergeant. Egan joined the Providence Police Department immediately after the war and by the turn of the century, he was the chief of the department. Egan was very prominent in the Rhode Island Irish-American community. This article provides interesting details regarding his service in the Third Rhode Island.

Metcalf, Edwin. *Personal Incidents in the Early Campaigns of the Third Regiment Rhode Island Volunteers and the Tenth Army Corps.* Providence: Sidney S. Rider, 1879.

Written by Metcalf, who later became the colonel of the Third Rhode Island, this volume covers the early history of the regiment and their conversion from an infantry to a heavy artillery regiment. Metcalf writes in detail about Newport's General Thomas West Sherman and his early war expedition to Hilton Head, South Carolina, where the bulk of the Third Rhode Island spent most of the war.

Williams, Alonzo. *The Investment of Fort Pulaski.* Providence: The Society, 1887.

The Siege of Fort Pulaski in April 1862 was the first action of the Third Rhode Island. Firing long range rifled guns against Confederate held Fort Pulaski near Savannah, Georgia, the Rhode Islanders destroyed the fort and proved the vulnerability of masonry forts, changing the face of warfare. This sketch recalls the actions of the Third Rhode Island in reducing the fort, and the types and numbers of cannons involved.

Fifth Rhode Island Heavy Artillery

Barney, C. Henry. *A Country Boy's First Three Months in the Army.* Providence: N. Bang Williams, 1880.

A native of Bristol, Barney served in Company A of the Fifth, and later became a lieutenant in the Fourteenth Rhode Island. In this publication, Barney chronicles the recruiting of the Fifth Rhode Island and his involvement in the Burnside Expedition. Barney writes about his participation at the Battle of New Bern and provides an eyewitness account of Kady Brownell at the battle.

Burlingame, John K. *History of the Fifth Regiment of Rhode Island Heavy Artillery During Three Years and a Half of Service in North Carolina. January 1862-June 1865.* Providence: Snow & Farnum, 1892.

The first published regimental history under the 1892 act, the Fifth Rhode Island was unique in that they spent their entire wartime service in North Carolina. The regiment spent most of the war on garrison duty and only engaged in occasional raids along the Carolina coast. Despite not being a "combat" regiment, this book is filled with interesting details regarding the Burnside Expedition, interactions with southern civilians in the New Bern area, as well as the prison experiences of those sent to Andersonville. The book is well illustrated with many engravings of both officers and men.

Chenery, William H. *Reminiscences of the Burnside Expedition.* Providence: The Society, 1905.

A lively account of the Burnside Expedition and the participation of the Fifth Rhode Island Heavy Artillery in the campaign. Chenery writes heavily regarding the terrible weather encountered by the expedition, as well as the Fifth's participation at New Bern and the Siege of Fort Macon.

Douglas, William W. *Relief of Washington, North Carolina by the Fifth Rhode Island Volunteers.* Providence: The Society, 1886.

As part of the Suffolk Campaign in the spring of 1863, a large Confederate force laid siege to Washington, North Carolina which was held by nine-month regiments from Massachusetts. To relieve the siege, the Fifth Rhode Island arrived and eventually the Confederates retired. To thank the Rhode Islanders, the men of the Forty-Fourth Massachusetts purchased an expensive regimental flag for the Fifth and later contributed to the large monument placed over the grave of Colonel Henry Sisson in Little Compton. This is a detailed sketch of the Fifth's role in this important, but forgotten engagement.

Hopkins, George C. "Battle of Newbern as I Saw it," in *Personal Recollection of the War of the Rebellion: Addressed Delivered Before the Commandery of the State of New York, Military Order of the Loyal Legion of the United States: Third Series.* Edited by Alexander Noel Blakeman. New York: Knickerbocker Press, 1907. Pp. 138-147.

Read before the New York Commandery of MOLLUS on December 7, 1898, Hopkins' paper chronicles the Battle of New

Bern on March 14, 1862 where the soldiers of the Fourth and Fifth Rhode Island Regiments played a major role in the Union victory. Hopkins gives a good overview of the engagement from the view of a company officer in the ranks and how the terrible weather affected Burnside's plans for the battle. His descriptions of the engagement are particularly useful.

Jervey, Edward D. *Prison Life Among the Rebels*. Kent: Kent State University Press, 1990.

This interesting volume is the memoirs of Chaplain Henry S. White of the Fifth Rhode Island. Visiting a fort at Croatan, North Carolina in April 1864, White and Company A of the Fifth who were manning the fort was captured by a large Confederate force. Nearly two thirds of the men in Company A died at Andersonville. Despite being a non-combatant, Chaplain White was still sent to prison. This book provides details of his experiences as a prisoner of war.

Underwood, Benjamin F. "The Burnside Expedition: Roanoke and Newbern." *The Narragansett Historical Register: Volume 9*. Pp. 1-36.

The adjutant of the Fifth Rhode Island during the Burnside Expedition, Underwood served in an important role during the campaign. He details the terrible weather encountered by the command, as well as the role played by the Fourth and Fifth Rhode Island in breaking the Confederate line at New Bern. A very informative article.

Fourteenth Rhode Island Heavy Artillery:

Addeman, Joshua M. *Reminiscences of Two Years with the Colored Troops*. Providence: N. Bang Williams, 1880.

A native New Zealander who went on to become Secretary of State for Rhode Island, Addeman also served in the Tenth Rhode Island for three months before becoming a captain in the

Fourteenth. In his reminiscences, he writes candidly about the realities of being a white officer in a black regiment and the fear of being captured by Confederate forces; white officers could and were executed for leading blacks. Addeman spent much of his service in Plaquemine, Louisiana and this sketch provides details of this service.

Brown, William J. *The Life of William J. Brown of Providence, R.I., with Personal Recollections of Incidents in Rhode Island.* Providence: Angell & Co., 1883.

The fascinating memoirs of a prominent member of Providence's black community, Brown wrote a detailed narrative of life in Providence in the mid nineteenth century. His memoirs provide detailed information regarding the recruiting of the Fourteenth and how the Civil War affected Rhode Island blacks.

Chenery, William H. *The Fourteenth Regiment Rhode Island Heavy Artillery (Colored), In the War to Preserve the Union, 1861-1865.* Providence: Snow & Farnum, 1898.

A comprehensive history of the Fourteenth, this book provides details of their service in Louisiana and Texas during the war. Chenery focused more on the white officer corps of the regiment, rather than the black enlisted men. As such, the book is filled with excellent biographical sketches of the officers, as well as many photographs.

Cottroll, Robert J. *The Afro-Yankees: Providence's Black Community in the Antebellum Era.* Westport: Greenwood Press, 1982.

A detailed social history of Providence's black community in the antebellum era. Cottroll writes about the struggles of blacks in Providence after they were freed from slavery. Also covered is the enfranchisement of Rhode Island black men following the Dorr Rebellion, their political activities, and how blacks sought employment in a white dominated city. An important work.

Grandchamp, Robert. *A Connecticut Yankee at War: The Life and Letters of George Lee Gaskell*. Gretna, LA: Pelican Publishing, 2015.

A highly revised edition of Grandchamp's 2010 M.A. thesis at Rhode Island College, this volume contains a biography, as well as the letters of Gaskell who served in both Battery G as a clerk and the Fourteenth Rhode Island as a lieutenant. Grandchamp includes additional letters written by Gaskell and focuses on his activities in Reconstruction era Louisiana. After his regiment was mustered out, Gaskell remained in Louisiana, married into a local Acadian family (he spoke fluent French and Latin), became a prominent politician and businessman, as well as an advocate for black rights. A well-researched book that is an important addition to the subject.

Naumec, David J. "From Mashantucket to Appomattox: The Native American veterans of the Connecticut and Rhode Island Colored Civil War Regiments." M.A. Thesis, Tufts University, 2004.

A very detailed look into members of the Narragansett, Niantic, and Pequot tribes that served in the Civil War. Several Narragansett tribal members are documented as serving in the Seventh Rhode Island; in the summer of 1862 Captain Rowland Gibson Rodman visited the reservation in Charlestown to recruit men for his company. More soldiers served in the Fourteenth Rhode Island Heavy Artillery. In Connecticut, the men served in the Twenty-ninth and Thirtieth Connecticut Volunteers, both regiments made up of black volunteers from that state.

Quinn, Edythe Ann. *Freedom Journey: Black Civil War Soldiers and The Hills Community, Westchester County, New York*. Albany: State University of New York Press, 2015.

The Fourteenth Rhode Island was composed of men recruited from throughout the North; only Companies A and B were composed primarily of Rhode Islanders. This book provides detailed information, as well as the letters of several Fourteenth

Rhode Island soldiers who served from New York. An informative study of black soldiers in the Civil War.

Saxbe, William B. "Bound for *Glory*: African-Americans from Rhode Island in the Massachusetts 54th and 55th Regiments, 1863-1865." *Rhode Island Roots* Vol. 39, No. 4 (December 2013), 207-210.

While the majority of black Rhode Islanders enlisted in the Fourteenth Rhode Island Heavy Artillery, five black Rhode Islanders joined the famous Fifty-Fourth Massachusetts and another five joined the Fifty-Fifth Massachusetts. Of the ten that joined, one was killed in action, and five died of disease, an appalling sixty percent death rate among these recruits. The article provides a list of these men and their fates.

Westwood, Howard C. "Company A of Rhode Island's Black Regiment: Its Enlisting, Its "Mutiny, Its Pay, Its Service." in *Black Troops, White Commanders, and Freedmen During the Civil War*. Carbondale: Southern Illinois University Press, 1992. Pp. 142-166.

Company A of the Fourteenth contained the majority of the native black Rhode Islanders, as well as some Narragansett Indians. This article, in an anthology of the role of black soldiers in the Civil War details the recruitment of Company A, as well as their service in Texas and Louisiana. When mustered for pay for the first time, the company nearly mutinied after not receiving the same pay as white soldiers. This article provides excellent information on the tumultuous relationship between white officers and black enlisted men in the Fourteenth Rhode Island.

Chapter Seven:

Cavalry Sources

First Rhode Island Cavalry

Bliss, George N. *Cavalry Service with General Sheridan, and Life in Libby Prison.* Providence: The Society, 1884.

Another of Bliss' many contributions to the Soldiers and Sailors Historical Society, this sketch recalls his service in the Shenandoah Valley in the summer and fall of 1864. Captured at Waynesboro after receiving a severe head wound, Bliss was saved after giving a secret Masonic word. He went on to spend several months in Libby Prison in Richmond. This is his narrative of that time.

Bliss, George N. *The First Rhode Island Cavalry at Middleburg, VA., June 17 and 18, 1863.* Providence: The Society, 1889.

One of the best sources of information regarding the destruction of the First Rhode Island Cavalry at Middleburg, Bliss places blame for the Rhode Islanders defeat squarely on the shoulders of Colonel Duffie. A highly detailed account of the battle, this text includes the reminiscences of several Rhode Island veterans, as well as a letter Bliss wrote the day after the battle. A very important resource.

Bliss, George N. *How I Lost My Sabre in War and Found it in Peace.* Providence: The Society, 1903.

Captain Bliss earned the Medal of Honor for his actions at Waynesboro in September 1864. This article relates his experiences in the battle, as well as how he lost his sabre in the engagement. After the war, Bliss befriended a member of the Virginia cavalry who opposed him at Waynesboro. This friendship led to the return of Bliss' sword after the battle. This sketch includes Bliss' correspondence with Confederate veterans.

Bliss, George N. *Prison Life of Lieut. James M. Fales.*
     Providence: N. Bang Williams, 1882.

Written by Fales and edited by Captain Bliss, this narrative relates Fales participation on the skirmish line at Middleburg and his experiences as a prisoner of war in Richmond following the battle.

Bliss, George N. *Reminiscences of Service in the First Rhode Island Cavalry.* Providence: Sidney S. Rider, 1878.

The first of Bliss' many contributions to the Soldiers and Sailors Historical Society, this sketch is a complete overview of his wartime experiences and does not delve into the detail of some of his later publications. A good overview of the life of a Union cavalryman.

Blumberg, Arnold. "My Poor Boys… All are Gone." *America's Civil War* (March 2017), 30-35.

This article is a direct plagiarism of Robert Grandchamp's 2007 article on the First Rhode Island Cavalry at Middleburg. A Baltimore attorney, Blumberg conducted no original research and copied direct from Grandchamp. A very poor article.

Cooke, Jacob B. *The Battle of Kelly's Ford, March 17, 1863.*
     Providence: The Society, 1887.

On March 17, 1863 at the Battle of Kelly's Ford, the First Rhode Island Cavalry was the first Union regiment to cross the river, leading a charge that demonstrated the fighting prowess of the Union cavalry, as well as earning a brigadier's star for Colonel Duffie. This detailed article recalls the role of the First Rhode Island in the battle and the losses they sustained there.

Denison, Frederic. *The Battle of Cedar Mountain: A Personal View. August 9, 1862.* Providence: N. Bang Williams, 1881.

The first major battle for the First Rhode Island Cavalry, Denison heavily chronicles the role of the First in the battle. This sketch includes much material not included in *Sabres and Spurs*.

Denison, Frederic. *The Battle of Groveton, August 28, 1862.* Providence: The Society, 1885.

Following the Battle of Cedar Mountain on August 9, 1862, the First Rhode Island Cavalry went on to see action in the Second Manassas Campaign in late August 1862. This sketch is Chaplain Denison's memoirs of that campaign.

Denison, Frederic. *Sabres and Spurs: The First Regiment Rhode Island Cavalry in the Civil War, 1861-1865. Its Origins, Marches, Scouts, Skirmishes, Raid, Battles, Sufferings, Victories, and Appropriate Official Papers; with The Roll of Honor and Roll of the Regiment.* Central Falls: E.L. Freeman, 1876.

One of the finest cavalry regimental histories, *Sabres and Spurs* was written by the regimental chaplain, Frederic Denison, who also wrote the history of the Third Rhode Island Heavy Artillery. Exceptionally well written, the book is filled with the personal narrative of the officers and men of the regiment, as well as Denison's wartime poetry. Serving throughout the war in the Army of the Potomac, the book heavily focuses on the role of the regiment in the Shenandoah Valley in 1862 and 1864, as well as the disastrous Battle of Middleburg. Of particular note is that the Third Battalion of the regiment was originally made up of soldiers from New Hampshire; these men later became the nucleus of the First New Hampshire Cavalry. As that regiment never had a history, *Sabres and Spurs* serves as the history of both.

Gardiner, William. *Incidents of Cavalry Experiences during General Pope's Campaign.* Providence: Sidney S. Rider, 1883.

A good narrative of the early campaigns of the First Rhode Island Cavalry. Gardiner includes information regarding Colonel Duffie's role in retraining the regiment, as well as their participation in the Second Manassas Campaign.

Gardiner, William. *Operations of the Cavalry Corps Middle Military Division, Armies of the United States from February 27 to March 8, 1865, Participated in by the First Rhode Island Cavalry.* Providence: The Society, 1896.

Reduced to a four company battalion following hard service in the Shenandoah Valley in 1864, the First Rhode Island Cavalry took part in Sheridan's final campaign in the Shenandoah Valley in the spring of 1865. Riding from Winchester, the army destroyed the vestiges of Confederate forces in the Valley, and then rode south to participate in the Appomattox Campaign; the Rhode Islanders were part of both campaigns. This narrative relates the experiences of the First Rhode Island in the spring of 1865.

Grandchamp, Robert. "Our Regiment has just been cleaned up: The First Rhode Island Cavalry at Middleburg." *Gettysburg Magazine* 37 (July 2007), 7-15.

An exceptionally well researched and detailed article about the June 17-18, 1863 engagement near Middleburg, Virginia in which nearly eighty percent of the First Rhode Island Cavalry became casualties. Grandchamp criticizes the Union command for sending the First Rhode Island unsupported behind enemy lines, as well as Colonel Duffie for not extracting his regiment in time.

Green, Charles O. *An Incident in the Battle of Middleburg, Va., June 17, 1863.* Providence: The Society, 1911.

On the night of June 17, 1863, the First Rhode Island Cavalry held the town of Middleburg, Virginia against an overwhelming Confederate force. Only after ammunition had been expanded and Confederate reinforcements arrived did the Rhode Islanders evacuate their barricades, only to be captured nearly to a man the following morning. This important sketch is Private Green's memoirs of the battle.

Guild, Emmons D. *500 Days in War Prisons: The Narrative of Emmons D. Guild of Attleboro, Massachusetts, who was captured October 12, 1863 in a detachment of the First Rhode Island Cavalry and thereafter was a captive in Culpepper, in an adjunct of Libby Prison at Richmond, in Belle Isle, in Andersonville, Millen, and Florence, S.C.* Attleboro: Daily Sun, 1935.

A very interesting and informative prison narrative from a soldier in the First Rhode Island Cavalry who survived Andersonville and several other southern prisons. Guild's narrative speaks of the horrors of prison life in the Civil War; his several escape attempts, and the many comrades he lost at Andersonville. The John Hay Library at Brown University contains many of Guild's wartime writings.

Leeds, Samuel Penniman. *Address at the funeral of Captain Lorenzo D. Gove, slain by the Rebels in Virginia, Delivered in the Congregational Church in Dartmouth College by S.P. Leeds.* Hanover: Dartmouth Press, 1863.

An interesting funeral sermon preached at Dartmouth College for Captain Gove of the New Hampshire Battalion of the First Rhode Island Cavalry. He was killed in action at Mountville, Virginia on October 31, 1862 and his remains were never recovered.

Longacre, Edward G. "Chaos Still Reigns in This Camp- Letters of Lieutenant George N. Bliss, 1st New England Cavalry, March-September 1862." *Rhode Island History* Vol. 36, No. 1 (February 1977), 15-24.

While Bliss published many writings regarding his service in the First Rhode Island Cavalry, his manuscript letters at the Rhode Island Historical Society are still an excellent source. This article is edited by Edward Longacre, a noted scholar on the cavalry of the Army of the Potomac. These interesting letters cover the early campaigning of the regiment in the Shenandoah Valley and the controversial appointment of Alfred N. Duffie to command the regiment.

Meyer, William E. *The Sailor on Horseback.* Providence: The Society, 1912.

Prior to joining the First Rhode Island Cavalry, Meyer had been a merchant sailor and had spent a large amount of time in the South at various ports. Meyer's narrative provides a good view of his prewar career as a sailor, as well as his experiences in the First Rhode Island Cavalry.

Stevens, Leverett C. *A Forlorn Hope.* Providence: The Society, 1903.

During the Battle of Middleburg, Stevens and several other men from the First Rhode Island Cavalry rode through Confederate lines to reach Union headquarters in an attempt to muster reinforcements to be sent to the aid of the embattled Rhode Islanders; none were sent and the result was the destruction of the regiment. This very important narrative recalls Stevens' ride on the night of June 17, 1863 and his experiences in the battle.

Wyman, Lillie Buffum Chase. *A Grand Army Man of Rhode Island.* Newton, MA: Graphic Press, 1925.

The detailed memoirs of Assistant Surgeon Augustine A. Mann of the First Rhode Island Cavalry. These memoirs provide a fascinating view of the actions of the First Rhode Island Cavalry at Middleburg, as well as Mann's subsequent imprisonment in Richmond.

Second Rhode Island Cavalry

Harrison, Donald Fisher. "A Unit History of the Second Rhode Island Cavalry 1862-1863." M.A. Thesis, University of Rhode Island, 1960.

The most important source for information on this neglected unit is Harrison's thesis, found at the University of Rhode Island. Expertly researched from a variety of primary sources including the official papers at the state archives, and newspaper sources, Harrison tells the full story of the Second Cavalry. Raised from bounty jumpers in the fall of 1862, the regiment suffered from desertion from the start. Sent to Louisiana, disease and picket duty took their toll and the regiment was disbanded in 1863. Also included are several detailed hand drawn maps. A very informative thesis that should have been published.

Morgan, Claude M. "Mutiny at Camp Hubbard." *Rhode Island History* Vol. 30, No. 4 (Fall 1971), 136-141.

After sustaining heavy losses to disease and desertion in 1863, the Second Rhode Island Cavalry was consolidated with the First Louisiana Cavalry. This event led to a mutiny among the Rhode Islanders in which two mutineers were executed without trial by the commander of the First Louisiana. This event led to an uproar in Rhode Island and a heated exchange between Governor James Y. Smith and the War Department. Eventually the survivors of the Second Cavalry were consolidated into two companies and transferred to the Third Rhode Island Cavalry.

Nelson, Chris. "Corliss is Back!" *Military Images* Vol. 24, No. 5 (March/April 2003), 34-35.

Nelson, Chris. "Harper's Ferry to Peking: The Journeys of a 19th Century Soldier: The Story of Brig. Gen. Augustus W. Corliss." *Military Images* Vol. 18, No. 4 (January-February 1997), 20-30.

A noted collector of military items, Nelson has amassed a large collection of material relating to Augustus W. Corliss who served as commander of the Seventh Squadron, as well as the Second Rhode Island Cavalry; he later served forty years in the Regular Army. Nelson's two articles are well researched, providing biographical material on Corliss, as well as illustrating photographs of him, and items Corliss used in the Civil War.

Sabre, Gilbert E. *Nineteen Months a Prisoner of War: Narrative of Lieutenant G. F. Sabre, Second Rhode Island Cavalry, of his experiences in the War Prisons and stockades of Morton, Mobile, Atlanta, Libby, Belle Island, Andersonville, Macon, Charleston, and Columbia, and his escape to the Union lines; to which is appended a list of officers confined at Columbia, during the winter of 1864 and 1865.* New York: The American News Company, 1865.

An interesting narrative written by an officer who was captured during the 1863 Port Hudson Campaign and spent most of the war as a prisoner. As with most prison narratives, the book chronicles the unimaginable hardships suffered by Union prisoners. The author wrote, "The scars remain forever the indelible marks of the terrible ordeal." The author of this book has never been fully identified. No Lieutenant Gilbert F. Sabre served in the Second Rhode Island Cavalry and the volume was written under an alias. Despite this, it is a good source of material for life in Confederate prisons.

Third Rhode Island Cavalry

Martin, Michael J. *The Wreck of the U.S. Transport North America.* Amery, WI: Bayonet Books, 2014.

While the Third Rhode Island Cavalry only lost a handful of men to enemy action in picket duty in the bayous of Louisiana, scores more died of tropical diseases. The worst loss to the regiment occurred on December 22, 1864 when over twenty members of the regiment drowned in the sinking of the *North America* off the coast of Georgia on their way home from the war after being discharged for disability. This thoroughly researched book is a very good account of the incident and includes information on the men of the Third Cavalry lost in the sinking.

Parkhurst, Charles H. *Incidents of Cavalry Service in Louisiana.* Providence: Sidney S. Rider, 1879.

Written by the second in command of the Third Rhode Island Cavalry, this is one of the few published resources available for the history of this unit. This interesting sketch provides good detail into the history of the Third Cavalry as they fought a guerilla war in the bayou country of Louisiana.

White, Frank F. Jr. "A Soldier Writes His Congressman: The Civil War Letters of Livingston Scott to Thomas A. Jenckes." *Rhode Island History* Vol. 18, No. 4 (October 1959), 97-113.

White, Frank F. Jr. "A Soldier Writes His Congressman: The Civil War Letters of Livingston Scott to Thomas A. Jenckes." *Rhode Island History* Vol. 19, No. 1 (January 1960), 13-25.

A detailed and fascinating set of letters written by Livingston Scott, a Brown University student to his congressman, Thomas A. Jenckes of Providence. Scott originally enlisted in the Tenth Rhode Island and served an uneventful three-month enlistment in the summer of 1862. He was commissioned into the Third Rhode Island Cavalry in 1863 and rose to captain. Scott's letters provide one of the best views into the history of this neglected unit, such as guerila fighting in the swamps of Louisiana, as well as various problems with the officer corps of the regiment. Scott frequently sought Jenckes assistance in obtaining a promotion, but it appears that Jenckes simply filed the letters away; the originals are in the Thomas A. Jenckes papers at the Library of Congress.

Seventh Squadron Rhode Island Cavalry

Alvord, Henry E. "A New England Boy in the Civil War," Edited by Caroline B. Sherman. *New England Quarterly V* (1932), 310-344.

A good set of letters from a member of the Seventh Squadron chronicling his decision to enlist as well as service in the Shenandoah Valley. Alvord went on to serve in the Second Massachusetts Cavalry, and his letters from that regiment are included as well. He later became president of what is now Oklahoma State University.

Corliss, Augustus W. *History of the Seventh Squadron, Rhode Island Cavalry*. Yarmouth, ME: "Old Times" Office," 1879.

A brief, but interesting history of the Seventh Squadron written by the unit commander, Major Corliss. This book includes the useful diary of Sergeant Henry Alvord as an appendix.

Ellis, William Arba. *Norwich University. Her History, Her Graduates, Her Roll of Honor*. Three Volumes. Concord: Rumford Press, 1898.

A superb three volume history of Norwich University, the book provides many details regarding the service of the Seventh Squadron, as well as providing biographies and photographs of all the members of Company B who came from Norwich University. In addition, several other Rhode Island officers had attended the school and Ellis' book provides biographies of them as well, among them was Major Jacob Babbitt of the Seventh Rhode Island who was mortally wounded at Fredericksburg.

Heysinger, Isaac W. "The Cavalry Column from Harper's Ferry in the Antietam Campaign." *Journal US Cavalry Association* (1914), 587-638.

An interesting first-person account of the cavalry expedition that escaped from Harpers Ferry shortly before the Union surrender on September 14-15, 1862 from Heysinger who was a student in the Seventh Squadron. He later served in the Regular Army and wrote a detailed history of the 1862 Maryland Campaign.

Nichols, William H. *The Siege and Capture of Harper's Ferry by the Confederates, September 1862.* Providence: The Society, 1889.

On September 14, 1862 nearly 12,000 Federal soldiers surrendered at Harpers Ferry to a large Confederate force under Stonewall Jackson. The night before the surrender, the Federal commander allowed his cavalry brigade to attempt to break through the Confederate lines and rejoin the Army of the Potomac; among those troops was the Seventh Squadron of Rhode Island Cavalry. This narrative, written by a member of Company A of the Squadron recalls the breakout and eventual capture of a Confederate wagon train.

Pettengill, Samuel B. *The College Cavaliers. A Sketch of the Service of a Company of College Students in the Union Army in 1862.* Chicago: H. McAllaster & Co., Printers, 1883.

The official history of the Seventh Squadron, this book covers the formation of this unique organization, as well as their service in the Shenandoah Valley in the summer of 1862. The book focuses exclusively on the exploits of the students of Company B of the unit; Company A was made up of men recruited in Rhode Island.

Chapter Eight:

Naval Sources

Avery, William B. *Gun-Boat Service on the James River.* Providence: The Society, 1884.

After resigning his commission in the New York Marine Artillery in June 1863, Avery became an ensign in the United States Navy. After receiving some brief training and seeing service during the New York Draft Riots, Avery served onboard various gun boats in the James River Squadron. This sketch provides interesting details regarding service along the coastal waterways during the Civil War. It is interesting to note that Avery preferred service in the army to the navy.

Avery, William B. *The Marine Artillery with the Burnside Expedition and the Battle of Camden, N.C.* Providence: N. Bang Williams, 1880.

A native of Providence and a veteran of the First Rhode Island Detached Militia, Avery served in the Burnside Expedition with the New York Marine Artillery, a unique organization that was not part of the United States Marine Corps. This sketch provides a detailed view of the Marine Artillery in the expedition; Avery earned the Medal of Honor for his actions at Tranter's Creek in June 1862.

Butts, Frank B. *A Cruise Along the Blockade.* Providence: The Society, 1881.

After being discharged from the navy in September 1863, Butts reenlisted shortly after as a paymaster's clerk aboard the *USS Flag*. These are his memoirs of his later war service as a member of the South Atlantic Blockading Squadron off Charleston, South Carolina as the vessel aimed to capture blockade runners.

Butts, Frank B. *The Monitor and the Merrimac.* Providence: The Society, 1890.

A detailed sketch of the most famous naval engagement of the Civil War, with particular attention paid to the construction and revolutionary design of the *Monitor.* It should be noted that during the engagement Butts was a private in Battery E and was not part of the crew, nor did he witness the engagement.

Butts, Frank B. *My First Cruise at Sea, and the Loss of the Iron-Clad Monitor.* Providence: Sidney S. Rider, 1878.

Originally a private in Battery E, Butts transferred to the Navy in the fall of 1862 and volunteered for service on the famed *USS Monitor.* Butts was onboard the *Monitor* when she sank off the Outer Banks in December 1862. One of twenty-eight survivors of the event, this is an important narrative of the sinking of the Union's most famous warship.

Butts, Frank B. *Reminiscences of Gun Boat Service on the Nansemond.* Providence: The Society, 1884.

After surviving the sinking of the *Monitor* with just the clothes on his back, Butts continued his service in the navy in 1863. This sketch chronicles his service on a gun boat in the Nansemond River Squadron near Suffolk, Virginia in 1863.

Badlam, William H. *Kearsarge and Alabama.* Providence: The Society, 1894.

A detailed account of the famous action off Cherbourg, France between the *USS Kearsarge* and the *CSS Alabama.*

Peet, Frederick Tomlinson. *Civil War Letters and Documents of Frederick Tomlinson Peet.* Newport: NP, 1917.

Peet, Frederick Tomlinson. *Personal Experiences in the Civil War.* New York: NP, 1905.

Frederick Tomlinson Peet was born in New York and served as an officer in Berdan's Sharpshooters. He was captured on the Virginia Peninsula in 1862 and after his release became an officer in the United States Marine Corps, serving in the South Atlantic Blockading Squadron. Although a New Yorker, Peet's family had a Newport connection and as such his books are included here. His letters and recollections are filled with interesting anecdotes about service on the Peninsula, his time in prison, and life as a Marine officer. The originals of the Peet material are housed at the Redwood Library in Newport, Rhode Island.

Pegram, John C. *Recollections of the United States Naval Academy.* Providence: The Society, 1891.

During the Civil War, the United States Naval Academy moved from Annapolis, Maryland to Newport, Rhode Island. In this sketch, written by a midshipman who attended the Academy while it was in Newport, Pegram discusses the reasons why the Academy was moved during the war, as well as the curriculum taught there. He also discusses the training of the midshipmen and life in Newport during the Civil War.

Chapter Nine:

Veteran Sources

Barber, John Michael. "Brotherhood: Abstracts of the Membership of Budlong Post No. 18, Grand Army of the Republic, Westerly, RI." *Rhode Island Roots* Vol. 27, No. 4 (December 2001), 153-186.

The local Grand Army of the Republic Post, Budlong Post met at the Westerly Public Library from the 1890s through the 1930s, today the records of the Post still reside at the library. In this detailed article, Barber has transcribed and analyzed the Post 18 roster books, providing a listing of the men who joined the post, as well as brief biographies of several members. Also included is a detailed bibliography of Budlong Post records available at the Westerly Public Library.

Ballou, Daniel Ross. *An Address: In Town Hall, Bristol, R.I., on Decoration Day, May 30, 1882.* Bristol: Bristol Phenix, 1882.

Delivered the year after the death of General Burnside, Ballou's address is an interesting Decoration Day address focusing on Burnside's career, while dedicating the new town hall in Bristol in his memory. Also includes a list of the Bristol soldiers who died in the Civil War.

Beath, Robert B. *History of the Grand Army of the Republic.* New York: Press of Willis McDonald & Co., 1888. Pp. 418-427.

This is a massive history of the Grand Army of the Republic published during the period in which the GAR saw its greatest number of members and attained its greatest political influence. The chapter on the history of the Department of Rhode Island is detailed and lists department officers and events within the department. The official records of the Department of Rhode Island of the Grand Army of the Republic, which existed from 1866 until 1943 are at the Rhode Island Historical Society in Providence.

Historical Sketch, Slocum Post, No. 10, Department of Rhode Island, G.A.R.: Chartered February 27th, 1868; Illustrated. Providence: Slocum Post, No. 10, 1894.

Named after the fallen colonel of the Second Rhode Island, Slocum Post 10 was the largest GAR Post in Rhode Island. This informative history provides a brief biography of Colonel Slocum, as well as a complete roster of all Post 10 officers and members from 1868 until 1894. Also included are photographs of each Post 10 commander, as well as a chronology of Slocum Post activities.

McGregor, Jeremiah S. *Life and Deeds of Dr. John McGregor: Including Scenes of His Childhood, Also Scenes on the Battle Field of Bull Run, at the Prisons in Richmond, Charleston, Castle Pinckney, Columbia, Salisbury, on the Banks of the James River, His Escape, His Return Home, the Tragical Scene on Dyer St., and the Heart-Rending Scene at the City Hotel in Providence, Where His Eventful Life Terminated.* Foster, R.I.: Press of Fry Bros, 1886.

A native of the western Coventry hamlet of Rice City, John McGregor served as the surgeon of the Third Connecticut Regiment and was captured at Bull Run. This volume is a biographical sketch of his life and service. McGregor died in 1867 and the GAR Post in Coventry was named in his honor.

Register of the Department of Rhode Island, Grand Army of the Republic, 1888. Providence: George H. Pettis, 1888.

A wonderful little volume, this is a roster of each member of the Department of Rhode Island in 1888, when GAR membership was at its peak. Each Post of the Department is listed, together with a membership and officer list of that Post. Each veteran is identified, as is the regiment they belonged to, and the community in which they resided. Also included is a listing of businesses in Providence owned by Civil War veterans. Unfortunately, unlike other departments, the 1888 roster was the only one published by the Department of Rhode Island. A very valuable resource.

Tobie, Edward P. *The Trip Down East, (To Auburn, ME) of Prescott Post, No. 1, Dept. of R.I. G.A. R.* Providence: J.A. & R.A. Reid, 1885.

In 1884, following the death of General Burnside and the organization of a GAR Post in Auburn, Maine named after Burnside, a large group of veterans traveled from Providence to dedicate a new GAR Hall in Auburn. This sketch, written by Tobie who served in the First Maine Cavalry and lived in Providence provides a detailed account of that trip.

Note: Each year, from 1866-1940, the Rhode Island Department of the Grand Army of the Republic published a set of *Proceedings of the Annual Encampment of the Department of Rhode Island Grand Arm of the Republic.* These report books provide detailed information regarding the Department, rosters of members, as well as officer reports. A very informative resource.

120

Chapter Ten:

Town Histories

Barrington

Bicknell, Thomas W. *A History of Barrington Rhode Island.*
    Providence: Snow & Farnum, 1898. Pp. 498-511.

A detailed history of Barrington written by a well-known local historian. Bicknell details the actions of the local town council during the conflict and includes a detailed roster of all the men from the town who served in the Civil War.

Bristol

Munro, Wilfred H. *The History of Bristol, R.I.: The Story of the
    Mount Hope Lands, From the Visit of the Northmen to
    the Present Time.* Pp. 358-362.

Book only includes a list of men from Bristol who volunteered. Munro acknowledged that the list was far from accurate as incomplete records were kept. Bristol was the adopted home of General Ambrose Burnside.

Coventry

Wood, Squire. *A History of Greene and Vicinity: 1845-1929.*
    Providence: NP, 1936. Pp. 38-41.

Much of Rhode Island west of Route 102 retains a distinct nineteenth century look, perhaps none more so than the village of Greene in western Coventry which is on the National Register of Historical Places. In this detailed history of Greene, Wood provides a detailed history of the area, and a list of Civil War veterans who enlisted from western Coventry.

East Greenwich

Greene, Daniel H. *History of the Town of East Greenwich and Adjacent Territory, From 1677 to 1877.* Providence: J.A. & R.A. Reid, 1877. Pp. 225-245.

Perhaps the most detailed of the early Rhode Island town histories, this history of East Greenwich includes two full chapters on the Civil War, focusing heavily on the role of the women of East Greenwich and their relief efforts to the town's soldiers. The book includes several letters written by local soldiers as well, adding to its value. Also included is information on the local militia unit, the Kentish Guards, many of its members saw service in the Second and Seventh Rhode Island Volunteers.

MacGunnigle, Bruce C. "Civil War Soldiers, Sailors, Marines, and Their Widows in East Greenwich, R.I. in 1890." *Rhode Island Roots* Vol. 42, No. 2 (June 2016), 91-100.

Widely published in the field of early Rhode Island history, MacGunnigle focused on East Greenwich Civil War veterans in this article. In 1890, the Federal government conducted a special census of all surviving Union veterans. MacGunnigle has transcribed the East Greenwich portion of the 1890 census and presents it here, adding additional information about the veterans, as well as several interesting photographs.

Exeter

Bell, Michael E. *Food for the Dead: On the Trail of New England's Vampires*. Middletown: Wesleyan University Press, 2011.

A very interesting cultural study about cultural beliefs in rural Rhode Island. In many rural communities until the 1890s, a widespread belief of vampirism existed, spurred on by periodic tuberculosis epidemics. Very useful to understand the cultural background of soldiers from the Exeter-West Greenwich-Coventry area.

Glocester

Kent, Edna. *Glocester: The Way Up Country.* Glocester: Glocester Bicentennial Commission, 1976. Pp. 45-54.

A detailed, readable history of Glocester published during the Bicentennial, Edna Kent, the town historian chronicles Glocester's participation in the Dorr Rebellion and the Civil War. Quoted in the work is a good letter from the Third Rhode Island Cavalry.

Hopkinton

Griswold, S.S. *Historical Sketch of the Town of Hopkinton, From 1757-1876, Comprising a Period of 119 Years.* Hope Valley: L.W.A. Cole, Job Printers, 1877. Pp. 46-51.

A small-town history, the few pages devoted to the Civil War list bounties paid by the town, as well as a roster of those who served. One out of every six men from Hopkinton died in the service, a casualty rate unseen in any Rhode Island town excepting South Kingstown.

Segar, Gladys and Betty Salomon. *Water Power Revisited: A Circle of Dam Sites Along the Wood and Pawcatuck Rivers.* Hope Valley: Langworthy Public Library, 1980.

Many of the men who enlisted from Richmond and Hopkinton were mill workers, employed in the many textile mills that sprung up in the 1840s and 1850s along the small streams of southwestern Rhode Island. This book provides excellent details into the many small mill villages that these men enlisted from, as well as photographs of the mills in the area.

New Shoreham

Dwyer, Michael F. "Some Civil War Soldiers from Block Island." *Rhode Island Roots* Vol. 38, No. 1 (March 2012), 28-32.

Although located off the coast of Rhode Island, the town of New Shoreham, located on Block Island sent her quota of men to the Civil War. In this interesting article, Dwyer presents detailed biographies and several photographs of soldiers who served from Block Island.

North Kingstown

Gardiner, George W. *Lafayette Rhode Island: A Few Phases of its History from the Ice Age to the Atomic.* Pawtucket: J.C. Hall Company, 1949.

An interesting local history of the village of Lafayette in North Kingstown. This book provides information on local Civil War veterans and focuses on George Cranston. A veteran of the Third Rhode Island, Cranston became a successful businessman and politician after the war. He served as Department Commander of the Grand Army of the Republic and the largest Civil War memorial in Rhode Island was erected in his honor in Elm Grove Cemetery in Wickford.

Providence

Collier, Theodore. "Providence in Civil War Days." *Rhode Island History* Vol. 27, No. 3 (July 1934), 66-83.

Collier, Theodore. "Providence in Civil War Days." *Rhode Island History* Vol. 27, No. 4 (October 1934), 98-113.

Two articles that provide an excellent view of Providence during the Civil War years. Collier writes in a lively style chronicling the mad rush to enlist in April 1861 as well as the reaction in Providence after the defeat at Bull Run. Also included are the actions of the Sanitary Commission and various businesses in the city as they produced war materiel. A very interesting article, unfortunately no sources are cited.

Garrett, Neysa Carpenter. "Sarah Bartlett Bullock, Part One: Reminiscences of Providence." *Rhode Island Roots* Vol. 43, No. 3 (September 2017), 115-123.

The reminiscences of a lifelong Providence resident, Bullock's memoirs provide insight into life on the East Side of Providence during the antebellum and Civil War eras. Bullock wrote, "My family was greatly opposed to the war, and our sympathies were strongly with the South." An interesting account written by a Rhode Island woman.

History of Providence County, Rhode Island: Volume I. Edited by Richard M. Bayles. New York: W.W. Preston & Co., 1891. Pp. 209-263.

A massive history of Providence County, this particularly long chapter provides excellent material regarding the happenings in the capital city during the Civil War. Also included are brief sketches on each Rhode Island regiment.

Richmond

Irish, James R. *Historical Sketch of the Town of Richmond, RI from 1747 to 1876, Comprising a Period of One Hundred and Twenty-nine years.* Hope Valley: L.W.A. Cole, printers, 1877. Pp. 64-67.

A thumbnail sketch of Richmond, this book gives a brief list of those who served from the town.

Scituate

Jones, Daniel P. *The Economic & Social Transformation of Rural Rhode Island, 1780-1850.* Boston: Northeastern University Press, 1992.

One of the finest books ever written on Rhode Island, this book provides a detailed analysis of rural north-western Rhode Island from the period after the Revolution to before the Civil War. Jones used many local sources to chronicle the religious, economic, and cultural activities of the inhabitants of the area. A very, very useful study to understanding the cultural background of the soldiers from Burrillville, Foster, Glocester, and Scituate.

Smithfield

Steere, Thomas. *History of the Town of Smithfield from its Organization in 1730-1, to its Division in 1871.*
   Providence: E.L. Freeman & Co., 1881. Pp. 209-220.

It must be remembered that during the Civil War, Smithfield was a much larger town and encompassed what is today the towns of Woonsocket, Smithfield, North Smithfield, Lincoln, and Central Falls. Book provides a roster of soldiers by regiment. The early records of Smithfield are kept at the Central Falls City Hall.

South Kingstown

McBurney, Christian M. *A History of Kingston, R.I., 1700-1900: Heart of Rural South County.* Kingston: Pettaquamscutt Historical Society, 2004. Pp. 253-261.

A masterfully researched and written history of the village of Kingston in South Kingstown, McBurnery, a native of the area and a prominent historian writes a detailed history of this community. He writes about the political and cultural activities in Kingston, the anti-slavery movement, as well as prominent locals. McBurney chronicles several locals who served in the conflict, including General Isaac Peace Rodman. A model town history.

Steadman, Daniel. *Daniel Steadman's Journal: 1826-1859.*
   Edited by Cherry Fletcher Bamberg. Greenville: Rhode Island Genealogical Society, 2003.

A detailed journal written by a farmer in South Kingstown in the years leading up to the Civil War, Steadman's diary provides a wealth of details regarding farming, social conditions, and the changing face of life in South County. Many neighbors and friends are mentioned, some of whom went on the serve in the Civil War.

Voices From the Civil War: Letters and Journal Excerpts of South Kingstown Men in the Union Army, 1861-1863. Edited by Shirley L. Barrett. South Kingstown: Pettaquamscutt Historical Society, 1992.

A very interesting and informative work that was published by the Pettaquamscutt Historical Society of South Kingstown; the society has a remarkable collection including items from Brigadier General Isaac Peace Rodman. This collection of writings includes letters and diary excerpts from Patrick Lyons who served in Company E of the Second Rhode Island Volunteers until he was severely wounded at the Wilderness. Also included are the letters of First Sergeant John K. Hull. A teacher, Hull served in Company G of the Seventh Rhode Island Volunteers and was killed at Jackson, Mississippi on July 13, 1863. A very informative book.

Warwick

Fuller, Oliver P. *The History of Warwick, Rhode Island, Settlement in 1642 to the Present Time*. Providence: Angell, Burlingame, & Co., Printers, 1875. Pp. 270-293.

In the Civil War era, Warwick included the town of West Warwick. Largely a rural farming community in the eastern half of the town, the western half was dominated by the many small mill villages along the Pawtuxet River. This book includes a list of each volunteer, the regiment in which they served, and their fate.

Johnson, Curt. *Speech Given by Curt Johnson at the Memorial Tribute to Rhode Island Civil War Troops Sunday, May 26, 1985*. Warwick: Warwick Historical Society, 1985.

A Memorial Day address that was later published by the Warwick Historical Society.

Westerly

Coy, Sallie E. *Westerly's Living Memorial.* Westerly: Utter Company, 1976.

The largest Civil War memorial in Rhode Island, the Westerly Public Library was dedicated in 1892 to the Civil War veterans of Westerly and neighboring Pawcatuck, Connecticut. For nearly forty years, the veterans of Budlong Post met there. This booklet is a detailed history of the Westerly Public Library. The Post meeting room still exists, while many GAR and Civil War records still exists in the collection.

Denison, Frederic. *Westerly (Rhode Island) and Its Witnesses, For Two Hundred and Fifty Years, 1626-1876. Including Charlestown, Hopkinton, and Richmond, until their Separate Organization, with the Principal Points of their Subsequent History.* Providence: J.A. & R.A. Reid, 1878. Pp. 269-273.

Denison, a native of Westerly served in the Civil War as chaplain of the First Rhode Island Cavalry and Third Rhode Island Heavy Artillery. A gifted historian, he wrote one of the better early town histories of Rhode Island. He wrote, "In every hour of our country's trial the inhabitants of Westerly have been prompt to pledge their honor and their blood." His brief chapter on the Civil War includes a list of those who served and died.

Dowding, George R. *Military History of Westerly 1710-1932.* Westerly: Blackburn & Benson, Printers, 1932.

Written by a World War I veteran, this booklet tells the story of Westerly through the various militia organizations raised in the town. Dowding focuses on the history of the Westerly Rifles, a militia unit twice activated for field service in the Civil War and which remains in service in the Rhode Island National Guard as the 169th Military Police Company.

Grandchamp, Robert. "Genealogical Resources of Southern Rhode Island." *American Ancestors* Vol. 10, No. 4 (Fall 2009), 43-45.

An in-depth analysis of local historical societies and libraries in South County, many of which contain Civil War collections.

Holman, Cindy Anderson. *Milltown Militia: North Stonington "Volunteers" in the Civil War*. North Stonington: C.A. Holman, 1986.

Bordering Westerly and Hopkinton, many North Stonington men served in Rhode Island units during the Civil War. This detailed study provides an excellent view of the town during the war. Holman includes several interesting photographs, as well as a roster of those who served. This book provides a good understanding of the men who crossed the state line to join Rhode Island regiments.

Shea, Robert F. "Aspects of the History of Westerly During the Civil War." M.A. Thesis, University of Rhode Island, 1957.

An above average M.A. Thesis, Shea covers many aspects of Westerly during the Civil War. He focuses on the men of Company I of the First Rhode Island Detached Militia and their early war service. Also covered are recruiting efforts, the economic impact of the war on the local economy, and the development of Watch Hill as a summer resort during the war. Well researched from local sources, this is an informative read.

Woonsocket

Delisle, Paul P. "Franco-American Civil War Veterans in the Woonsocket, RI Area." *Je Me Souviens* Vol. 21, No. 1 (Spring 1998), 97-108.

A very detailed listing of Quebecois soldiers who resided in the Woonsocket area after the Civil War. Delisle provides short biographies of these men.

Richardson, Erastus. *History of Woonsocket.* Woonsocket: S. S. Foss, 1876. Pp. 105-120.

Woonsocket erected the first Civil War monument in Rhode Island in 1867, only two years after the war ended. This book includes a detailed history of the Woonsocket Guards, which served in the Civil War as Company K, First Rhode Island Detached Militia, as well as a roster of the men from the community who served in the war. During the Civil War, Woonsocket was a large mill village that was technically part of the towns of Cumberland and Smithfield, divided by the Blackstone River. The town was incorporated in 1867 and later became a city. The first Rhode Islander to die in the Civil War, Private Henry C. Davis came from Woonsocket.

Chapter Eleven:

Monuments and Cemeteries

Burgess, Gideon A. *The Owen Soldier's Monument North Scituate, R.I.: Dedicated August 20, 1913.* North Scituate: E.F. Sibley & Co., 1913.

Dedicated in 1913, the Civil War monument in Scituate was one of the last to be dedicated in Rhode Island. This very detailed sketch, published for the dedication ceremony provides detailed information regarding the role of Scituate in the Civil War, as well as providing details and a list of the men from Scituate who died in the army.

Chevalier, R.N. and Donna Chevalier. *Rhode Island Civil War Monuments: A Pictorial Guide.* Glocester: Stillwater River Publications, 2017.

This interesting book provides color photographs of all known Civil War monuments in Rhode Island. The authors have done a tremendous job in taking up close images of many of the minute details on the state's Civil War memorials. A good book.

"Dedication of the Soldiers and Sailors Monument at Riverside Cemetery South Kingstown, R.I., June 10, 1886." *The Narragansett Historical Register: Volume 5.* Pp. 81-125.

Proportionally no town lost more men than South Kingstown; one out of every three men who served in the Seventh Rhode Island and the losses were equal in other units. This sketch, which was also later published as a separate pamphlet chronicles the efforts to build a memorial to the soldiers of South Kingstown. The planning for the monument is included, as are the dedication exercises, and a list of the men from the town who died in the war.

Grand Army of the Republic. *Memorial of Col. John Stanton Slocum, First Colonel of the Second Rhode Island Volunteers, Who Fell in the Battle of Bull Run, Va., July 21, 1861*. Providence: J.A. & R.A. Reid, 1886.

This volume is a biographical sketch of Colonel Slocum, as well as providing information regarding the monument erected to his memory at Swan Point Cemetery. The proceedings of the dedication of the monument are also included. The best source of material for information about Colonel Slocum.

Grandchamp, Robert. "Rhode Island Civil War Soldiers Buried at Antietam." *Rhode Island Roots* Vol. 34, No. 1 (March 2008), 38-40.

A compilation of the Rhode Island soldiers buried at Antietam National Cemetery in Sharpsburg, Maryland.

Grandchamp, Robert and Joyce Knight Townsend. "Rhode Island Civil War Soldiers Buried at the National Cemetery, Togus, Maine." *Rhode Island Roots* Vol. 43, No. 3 (September 2017), 160-168.

Founded immediately after the Civil War as the first National Soldier's Home, the facility in central Maine became a haven for disabled and retired Civil War soldiers and continues in operation as a Veterans Affairs hospital today. This article traces the development of Togus site, why Rhode Island veterans went there, as well as providing a list of the 150 Rhode Island soldiers buried at the site.

Grandchamp, Robert. "Rhode Island Civil War Dead Buried in the South." *Rhode Island Roots* Vol. 34, No. 3 (September 2008), 138-141.

Grandchamp, Robert. "More of Rhode Island's Civil War Dead." *Rhode Island Roots* Vol. 35, No. 3 (September 2009), 154-159.

Two articles containing transcriptions of Rhode Island Civil War soldiers buried in some of the smaller national cemeteries in the South.

Matthew, Linda L. "Rhode Islanders Buried in New Bern, N.C." *Rhode Island Roots* Vol. 21, No. 2 (June 1995), 41-43.

A compilation of the Rhode Island soldiers buried at New Bern National Cemetery in New Bern, North Carolina. These men served in the Fourth and Fifth Rhode Island, as well as Battery F.

Outdoor Sculpture of Rhode Island. Providence: Rhode Island Historical Preservation and Heritage Commission, 1999.

Civil War monuments are found in most Rhode Island communities. This book is a detailed survey of all outdoor sculpture found in Rhode Island and documents the history of these monuments. Provides interesting details on the history of public commemoration in Rhode Island, as well as identifying some of the smaller, forgotten monuments, such as the memorial to Colonel Henry Sisson in Little Compton.

Rogers, Horatio. *Record of the Rhode Island Excursion to Gettysburg, October 11-16, 1886: With the Dedicatory Services of the Battlefield Memorials of the Second Rhode Island Volunteers, and Batteries A and B, First R.I. Light Artillery.* Providence: E.L. Freeman & Son, 1887.

In October of 1886, the veterans of Batteries A and B, as well as the Second Rhode Island Volunteers returned to Gettysburg to dedicate a monument to each unit. This book provides a detailed look at the creation, erection, and dedication of those monuments, as well as the Gettysburg reminiscences of several veterans. A good source for information on the Battle of Gettysburg

Woodbury, Augustus, and Sarah Helen Whitman. *Proceedings at the Dedication of the Soldiers' and Sailors' Monument: Erected in Providence by the State of Rhode Island: with the Oration by the Rev. Augustus Woodbury, and the Memorial Hymn by Mrs. Sarah Helen Whitman: to Which Is Appended a List of the Deceased Soldiers and Sailors Whose Names Are Sculptured Upon the Monument.* Providence: A. Crawford Greene, 1871.

Erected in Exchange Place in Providence in 1871, the Rhode Island Soldiers and Sailors Monument is the state's official Civil War memorial. On the large monument are engraved the names of every known Rhode Islander who died in the Civil War at that time, although current research indicates that more names should be on the monument. This book chronicles the building of the monument, as well as providing a detailed report of the dedication services. In addition, it includes a list of the names on the monument. A very important volume.

Chapter Twelve:

Conclusions

From 1861-1865 nearly 24,000 men enlisted in Rhode Island to serve in the Civil War. In the decades after, these veterans published dozens of accounts and left behind an invaluable written record for future historians. These veteran written accounts have been supplemented by dozens more books, articles, and other publications about Rhode Island's role in the Civil War. As can be seen in the pages above, Rhode Islanders have truly left behind a lasting legacy in print. What then, does the future hold?

Unfortunately, the future does not appear bright for continued publications about Rhode Island and the Civil War. While the veterans who took part in the conflict wanted their story told and often wrote about it through the publications of the Soldiers and Sailors Historical Society, or in state sponsored regimental histories, current scholarship in the field is limited to two active participants, while academia often does not view the study of Civil War military history in the best light.

The Civil War Sesquicentennial commemorated from 2011-2015 was a litmus test for Rhode Island that unfortunately the state failed at. While other states such as Virginia, South Carolina, Maine, and notably Connecticut supported and funded commissions to organize events and publications, Rhode Island only organized a group in February 2011. Led by noted Lincoln scholar and retired Chief Justice Frank Williams, the twenty-seven-member commission, comprised of Rhode Islanders from a wide array of backgrounds published a lofty mission statement:

> The Commission and its advisory council will explore and publicize this important history – military, political, and cultural – in a myriad of ways during the years 2011 through 2015. We will support projects to restore Civil

War monuments and to digitize Civil War related data; we will endorse reenactments and exhibits, expand this website, and produce publications; and we will devote much energy to the education of our citizens – especially students – about this crucial era of our history. The volunteer efforts of the Commission, its advisory council, supportive educators, and Rhode Island citizens in general – all without remuneration – will strive to meet these goals.

Unfortunately, few, if any of these goals were met. While a website was created by the commission and they did include some images of Rhode Island soldiers, and some events were listed, the website did not accomplish much, in comparison to neighboring Connecticut which frequently updated with events taking place all through the Nutmeg State. The twenty-seven-member committee proved to be unwieldly, while the Rhode Island General Assembly did not fund the commission's work; instead they had to rely on donations to remain active.

In April 2011, a group of Rhode Islanders met at the Benefit Street Arsenal to commemorate 150 years since the Providence Marine Corps of Artillery left the building as one of the first groups of northern militia to respond to Lincoln's call for volunteers. Four years later, another ceremony was held at the arsenal to commemorate the end of the war and to dedicate a plaque to the seven soldiers of Battery G who earned the Medal of Honor at Petersburg on April 2, 1865. With the exception of the annual Fort Adams reenactment, and Rhode Island Day at Antietam National Battlefield, neither event being sponsored by the commission, few events transpired in Rhode Island during the sesquicentennial.

While Connecticut sponsored an official sesquicentennial history of Nutmeg State participation, Rhode Island did not. Rather, the Rhode Island Sesquicentennial Commission secured a small grant to publish *The Rhode Island Homefront in the Civil War Era,* a compilation of essays regarding economic, social, and political events in Rhode Island. Sam Simons published a well-received series of bi-weekly articles in *The Westerly Sun* from 2012-2013, but even these were only read locally in South County. A planned one-day symposium in April 2014 was canceled due to lack of pre-registration. Unfortunately, in the end, the Civil War Sesquicentennial was a failure in Rhode Island and did not generate the interest in the conflict that was created in other states.

Why, unlike other states, is the Civil War often placed on the backburner in Rhode Island? In Maine, one can walk into the stately home of war hero General Joshua Lawrence Chamberlain; in Connecticut one can visit the restored Grand Army of the Republic Hall in Rockville, now home to the New England Civil War Museum. Lebanon, New Hampshire also boasts a restored GAR Hall, while a visitor can drive to many historical sites in Vermont, including the American Precision Museum in Windsor which was originally a musket manufacturing center. In Rhode Island, with the exception of Fort Adams and the Westerly Public Library, once a GAR Hall, few, if any tangible sites remain in Rhode Island relating to the Civil War. Furthermore, much of the state's vast history is stored away in archival boxes at Brown University, the Rhode Island Historical Society, and the Rhode Island State Archives. With the exception of the magnificent Varnum Continentals collection in East Greenwich, there is not a major museum in the state dedicated to Rhode Island's rich military history.

There are two major reasons why Rhode Island Civil War history is not front and center. Rhode Island is very much a "melting pot" state. As each new ethnic group comes into Rhode Island, they do not look to the deeds of the past. The Irish and Quebecois were active participants in the Civil War experience in Rhode Island, however as they were supplemented by the Italians, in turn by Latinos and East Asians, each new group, while bringing much and contributing to the vitality of Rhode Island, has not embraced the rich historical past of Rhode Island. One only need to look at the Soldiers and Sailors Monument in Providence; Rhode Island's version of the Vietnam Wall to understand this. The monument is frequently covered in pigeon excrement, while vagabonds sleep, and transients sit wild eyed on this sacred place to commemorate Rhode Islanders who gave "the last full measure of devotion."

In addition, Rhode Island history is not, for the most part, an academic discipline. With the retirement of Patrick Conley from Providence College, and Stanley Lemons from Rhode Island College, the state lost two of the best academics in the field of Rhode Island history that were not replaced with equal peers in the field. While Rhode Island College, the University of Rhode Island, and others teach Rhode Island history classes, they are general survey courses, not in-depth studies. Also inhibiting is the lack of an academic press attached to a university or college in Rhode Island publishing books about the rich history of the state. When academics do study Rhode Island history it is largely the colonial period, or Rhode Island's notorious involvement in the Triangle Trade. Even the Fourteenth Rhode Island Heavy Artillery, a black regiment, has not received the academic treatment of the neighboring Fifty-Fourth Massachusetts. A lack of education about Rhode Island history, coupled with a disregard of the state's history have all contributed to Rhode Island Civil War history being neglected.

In conclusion, the history of Rhode Island and the Civil War must continue to be studied. The Civil War was and remains the defining moment in American history. Rhode Islanders left an indelible mark on the battlefield and in the pages of the history they wrote. It waits to be seen if future generations will pick up the pen and continue writing about the noble deeds they achieved.

Acknowledgements

First and foremost, although they are no longer with us, I must thank the veterans of Rhode Island's Civil War units for leaving behind such a rich legacy of their service in print. Although some sources were very difficult to find, these writings provide a fantastic, detailed view into the service of the men from Rhode Island in the Civil War. Equally, I must thank the Rhode Island General Assembly. By sponsoring the 1892 regimental history legislation, they provided the veterans and future historians a lasting gift by allowing these regimental histories to be published.

At the Rhode Island State Archives, Ken Carlson was instrumental in finding many of the smaller government publications. As always, Kris VanDenBossche pointed me in the path of some of the smaller sources and provided access to his wonderful collection.

Retired Chief Justice Frank Williams is to be commended for his leadership of the Rhode Island Civil War Sesquicentennial Commission. Rhode Island owes Chief Williams a debt of gratitude for helping keep Civil War history alive in the Ocean State.

In Providence, General Richard Valente provided access to the Benefit Street Arsenal and its vast resources while I was working on the book *Rhody Redlegs*. The staffs at the Rhode Island Historical Society, Providence City Hall Archives, Brown University, and the Providence Public Library were equally helpful.

Captain Phil DiMaria of Battery B has been a mentor, friend, and guide for nearly twenty years as I navigated and researched the role of Rhode Island in the Civil War era. Without Phil's assistance and guidance, none of this work would have been possible.

Nina Wright and the staff at the Westerly Public Library always provided access and many photocopies when I visited that wonderful institution, as did Matt Reardon of the New England Civil War Museum in Rockville, Connecticut.

At the Varnum Continentals, Patrick Donovan provided access to the collections and listened to my many stories.

Cherry Fletcher Bamberg of the Rhode Island Genealogical Society is to be commended to guiding my research and writing over the years as I wrote many articles for *Rhode Island Roots*.

Master Sergeant Jim Loffler, the historical section chief of the Rhode Island National Guard was helpful in tracking down some interesting Dorr Rebellion sources. Russell DeSimone and Christian McBurney were also helpful in this department.

Although many years have passed, the interlibrary loan staff and Marlene Lopes at Rhode Island College Special Collections will always be remembered for their assistance in finding long lost books and articles while I was a student there from 2004-2010.

Many of these sources were found in various repositories throughout Rhode Island and although I may not have remembered names, I do wish to thank these institutions that assisted in this work: Langworthy Public Library, East Providence Historical Society, Foster Preservation Society, Scituate Preservation Society, Newport Historical Society, Redwood Library, Burrillville Historical and Preservation Society, Glocester Heritage Society, Bristol Historical Society, North Kingstown Public Library, East Greenwich Public Library, Westerly Armory Foundation, and the South County Museum.

Lastly, I must thank my dear wife Elizabeth. She has the patience of a saint and gladly lives with the Civil War every day.

ABOUT THE AUTHOR

Robert Grandchamp first became interested in the Seventh Rhode Island Volunteers in 2001, after learning from his grandmother that his third great uncle, Alfred Sheldon Knight had served in the regiment as a private in Company C and died of pneumonia serving in the Civil War. Robert became very interested in the Civil War in general at this time, and began to read frequently about the Seventh and its campaigns. Trips to battlefields, libraries, and archives fueled his interest and he soon began to collect material for a regimental history that was published in 2008 as *The Seventh Rhode Island Infantry in the Civil War.* Among his other works are *Rhody Redlegs, The Boys of Adams' Battery G, Colonel Edward E. Cross, Rhode Island and the Civil War: Voices from the Ocean State,* and *A Connecticut Yankee at War: The Life and Letters of George Lee Gaskell.* Robert earned his M.A. in American history from Rhode Island College, in addition to his B.A. in anthropology and American history from Rhode Island College as well. He is a former National Park Ranger with service at Shenandoah and Harpers Ferry battlefield. For his efforts to honor the soldiers from Rhode Island, Robert has been awarded the Order of Saint Barbara from the Rhode Island National Guard, the Margaret B. Stillwell Prize from the John Russell Bartlett Society at Brown University, as well as letters of commendation from the governor of Rhode Island and mayor of Providence. Among his professional affiliations, he is a longtime member of several historical organizations, including the Rhode Island Genealogical Society. Robert is an analyst with the Federal government and resides with his wife Elizabeth in Jericho Center, Vermont.

www.ingramcontent.com/pod-product-compliance
Lightning Source LLC
Chambersburg PA
CBHW050642160426
43194CB00010B/1781